Three Faces Of Noir

Curse Crime Cringe

Film Noir In The Public Domain Vol IV

Three Faces Of Noir
Curse Crime Cringe
Film Noir In The Public Domain Vol IV

First edition published in Australia in 2025 by

Bent Banana Books

24 Lorraine Court

Lawnton, Australia, 4501.

Email bentbananabooks@gmail.com

All characters are fictitious and any resemblance to actual persons living, or dead is purely coincidental.

Cover and layout designer: Bernardos!

ISBN: 978-1-7638100-3-7 Paperback

A CiP catalogue record for this book is available from the Australian National Library.

About the author

Bernie Dowling is an Australian writer working in journalism, fiction, and non-fiction.

His first novel is the neo-noir *Iraqi Icicle*. His non-fiction *Maaate! Bribe Proofing The Public Purse Against Good Blokes* is about corruption in local government.

The author is publishing a four-book series on film noir in the public domain. The first volume *Noir Dirt Cheap* was published in 2023. *Film Noir Fate Vs The Working Stiff* appeared in 2024. *Starry Starry Noir Rebels And Censors* was published in 2025.

Three Faces Of Noir

Curse Crime Cringe

Film Noir In The Public Domain Vol IV

Let any pretty girl announce a divorce in Hollywood and the wolves come running. Fresh meat for the beast, and they are always hungry.
– Hedy Lamarr

In memory of
Joseph Calleia,
an acting giant
big on Broadway, and
small on the big screen.

Introduction

HARRY H. **CORBETT**   DIANE **CILENTO**

RATTLE OF A SIMPLE MAN

1964

I have a simple understanding of the seedlings of film noir, a most contentious genre. Right now, I can hear readers yelling at this page, "It's not a genre." I am not buying into that debate.

In my simple view, noir evolved over two decades from its birth in German Expressionist film, a style developed after World War I in reaction to the horrors of the war. Three of the great noir novelists – Dashiell Hammett, Raymond Chandler, and James M. Cain – were seriously injured during what was perversely called the Great War.

Cain was not drafted until June 1918. He volunteered for the front lines in France and was almost killed by poison gas.

Battles in France and Belgium between German and Allied troops were horrendous. The Battle of the Somme was fought in northern France from July to November 1916 when British and French troops tried to overpower German trench lines.

Casualties: The British made a propaganda film about the Battle of the Somme. The doco screened in August 2016, barely a month into the battle.

The British called off the offensive after five months. British and French casualties – dead and wounded – were 620,000. German casualties were estimated at upwards of 450,000. During the five months, the Allied troops had gained ground of seven miles (12km).

Allied casualties and the uninjured suffered shell shock, as post-traumatic stress disorder (PTSD) was then called. By 1917, defense command banned shell shock as a medical term.

BILL **WILLIAMS** · BARBARA **HALE**
THE CLAY PIGEON

Amnesia: In this 1949 noir, an amnesiac wakes up in hospital to learn he is accused of murder.

A symptom of shell shock was amnesia, also a popular device in noir. As late as 2000, the inventive neo-noir *Memento* was still using amnesia as its basic device

Desertion or being absent without leave (AWOL) were capital offenses during WWI. The 306 British and Commonwealth soldiers shot at dawn included teenagers.

Discernibly noir: *Stranger on the Third Floor.*

I agree with the utility of crediting *Stranger on the Third Floor* 1940 as Hollywood's first noir. The lead player Peter Lorre was Hungarian born, the director Boris Ingster was Russian born, the co-writer Frank Partos was Hungarian born, and the cinematographer Nicholas Musuraca was Italian born. The European influence on film noir is undeniable.

Nosferatu 1922 is often written without its subtitle: *A Symphony of Horrors*. Paul Wegener wrote the screenplay. The title is a critique of the pre-war Expressionist visual artists who were optimistic the war would overthrow the materialist and intolerant ruling class (Museum of Modern Art *Expressionist Depictions of War* online). Wegener also wrote the tale of hubris of people "in control" *The Golem: How He Came into the World* 1920, a precursor of Hollywood's *Frankenstein* 1931 though Mary Shelley wrote the source novel in the early 19th century.

1927

Thus Expressionists working in film and theater favored stories of horror and dystopia with matching askew and intimidating sets, and actors' expressions of pain and anguish.

The directors of *Nosferatu*, F.W. Murnau and *Metropolis* Fritz Lang, went to Hollywood.

F.W. Murnau's first American movie, the drama *A Song of Two Humans* 1927, was clearly Expressionist, in sets, photography and acting style. *A Song of Two Humans* won the award for Unique and Artistic Picture at the inaugural Academy Awards in 1929.

FURY

Lang's first Hollywood film was the striking proto-noir *Fury* 1936, starring Sylvia Sidney and Spencer Tracy. Again, the Expressionist influence is obvious.

Directors

PAUL LENI directed *Waxworks* 1924 in Germany, and, in Hollywood, *The Cat and the Canary* `1927, and *The Man Who Laughs* 1927.

CARL LAEMMLE presents
KARLOFF and BELA LUGOSI in
EDGAR ALLAN POE'S "The BLACK CAT"
with
DAVID MANNERS · JACQUELINE WELLS · LUCILLE LUND · EGON BRECHER · HARRY CORDING HENRY ARMETTA · ALBERT CONTI · LOUIS ALBERNI
A UNIVERSAL PICTURE

EDGAR G. ULMER was an Austrian set designer in Germany before he came to Hollywood where he made a string of B-noirs in the 1940s. But before these, Ulmer directed the surprise horror hit *The Black Cat* 1931. If you went up close, you could see the director's name on the poster.

Frenchman **JACQUES TOURNEUR** made the Hollywood B-horrors *Cat People* 1942, *I Walked with a Zombie* 1943, and *The Leopard Man* 1943 before the noir classic *Out of the Past* 1947.

European directors of Hollywood noir included Robert Siodmak, Billy Wilder, Fred Zinnemann, Michael Curtiz, Anatole Litvak, Otto Preminger, William Wyler, Lewis Milestone, André De Toth, Jean Negulesco, Rudolph Maté, Jean Renoir, Robert Florey, Max Ophüls, and Ida Lupino.

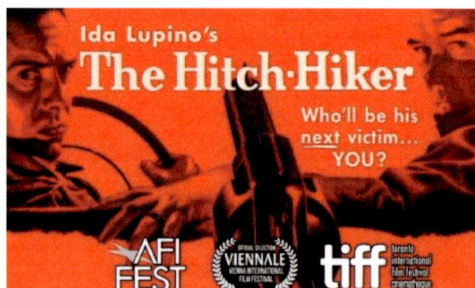

Ida Lupino's
The Hitch-Hiker
Who'll be his next victim... YOU?
AFI FEST · VIENNALE VIENNA INTERNATIONAL FILM FESTIVAL · tiff toronto international film festival cinémathèque

Cinematographers

KARL FREUND photographed *The Golem* and *Metropolis* before moving to the United States where Freund shot *Dracula* 1931, *Murders in the Rue Morgue* 1932, and *Key Largo* 1948.

Beware, Claire: Claire Trevor in *Raw Deal.*

Hungarian born **JOHN ALTON** produced amazing cinematography in B-noirs, often in co-operation with director Anthony Mann. Two awesome examples of the Alton talent are both from 1948 *He Walked by Night,* and *Raw Deal.*

Other Alton noirs are *T-Men* 1947, *The Amazing Mr. X* 1948, *Border Incident* 1949, *The Crooked Way* 1949, *Mystery Street* 1950, *Witness to Murder 1954,* and *The Big Combo* 1955.

Hungarian born **ERNEST LASZLO** was director of photography on a stack of noirs including the acclaimed titles *D.O.A.* 1950, *The Well* 1951, *The Big Knife* 1955, *Kiss Me Deadly* 1955, and *While the City Sleeps* 1956. Laszlo won the Academy Award for *Ship of Fools* 1965.

Combo: The band The Fishermen in *D.O.A.*

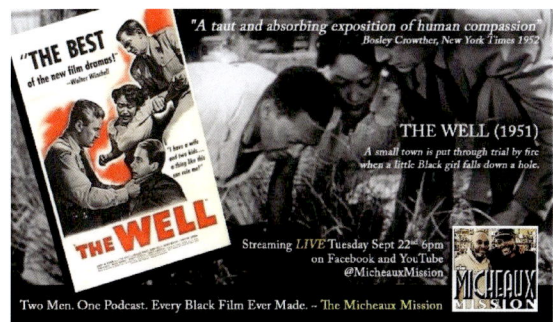

Race relations: The Well.

White Fang: That was the nickname of studio boss Harry Cohn. Rod Steiger had this hair style made up to portray a caricature of Cohn in *The Big Knife*.

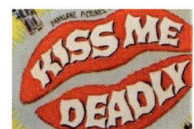

The Hungarian born director of *D.O.A.* **RUDOLPH MATÉ** was a cinematographer before he switched to directing. He photographed the French classic *The Passion of Joan of Arc* 1928, directed by Dane, Carl Theodor Dreyer. Maté shot *Vampyr* 1931, also directed by Dreyer.

In America, Maté shot the noir *Gilda* 1946, starring Rita Hayworth and Glenn Ford. He directed the noir *Union Station* 1950.

Legend: Renée Jeanne Falconetti as Joan of Arc.

Loser: Elisha Cook Jr. in *Stranger on the Third Floor*.

Italian born **NICHOLAS MUSURACA** photographed *Stranger on the Third Floor* 1940, *Cat People* 1942, *The Spiral Staircase* 1946, *The Locket* 1946, *Out of the Past* 1947, *Born to be Bad* 1950, *Clash by Night* 1952, *The Hitch-Hiker* 1953, and *The Blue Gardenia* 1953.

On a scored average for the quality of all his noirs, Musuraca would outpoint John Alton and James Wong Howe.

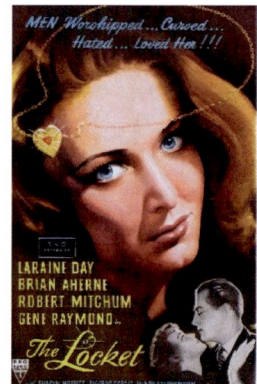

Hungarian expat **FRANZ PLANER** shot the underrated noir, *The Face Behind the Mask* 1941, *The Chase* 1946, *Criss Cross* 1949, *Champion* 1949, and *The Caine Mutiny* 1954.

Italian born Salvatore **"SOL" POLITO** shot the proto-noir *The Petrified Forest* 1936. It was one of the first Hollywood premises-invasion hostage noirs which became popular during the heyday of the Cold War in the 1950s. Sol Polito photographed the noir classic *Sorry Wrong Number* 1948 (When I say photographer I mean director of photography. The DI might operate the camera for part or even none of the filming).

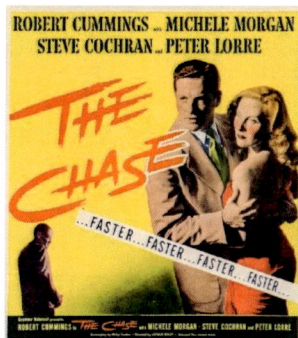

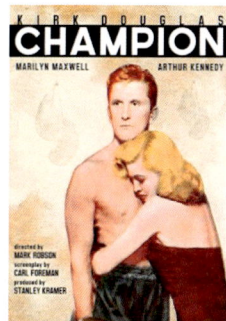

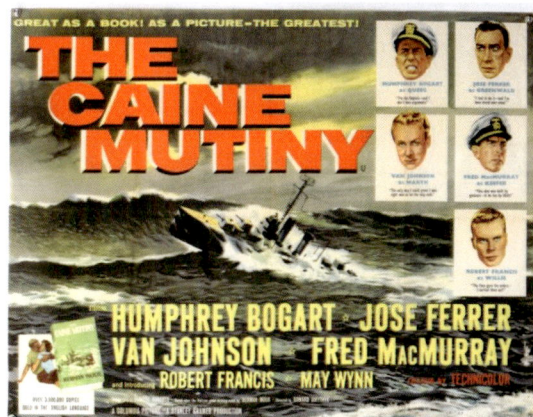

Musical directors

Austrian born **MAX STEINER** wrote more than 300 film scores. As Steiner often worked with RKO and Warners, quite a few were for noirs. He won an Academy Award for the proto-noir *The Informer* 1935. His noirs included *Mildred Pierce* 1945, *The Big Sleep* 1946, *Key Largo* 1948, and *White Heat* 1949.

Light and shade: Wallace Ford in *The Informer*.

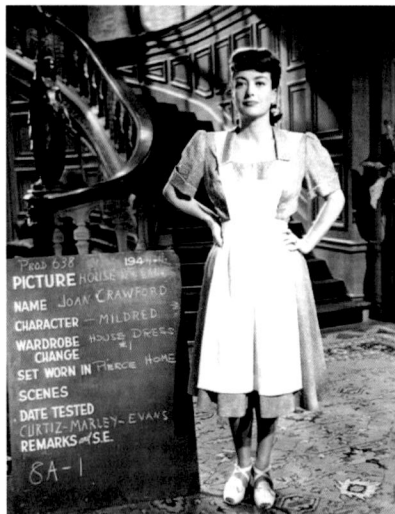

Smart change: The working title for *Mildred Pierce* was *House on the Sand*.

German **FRANZ WAXMAN** scored *Bride of Frankenstein* 1935, proto-noir *Fury* 1936, and *Rebecca* 1940. Waxman did the music for *Sunset Boulevard* 1950, and *Night and the City* 1950.

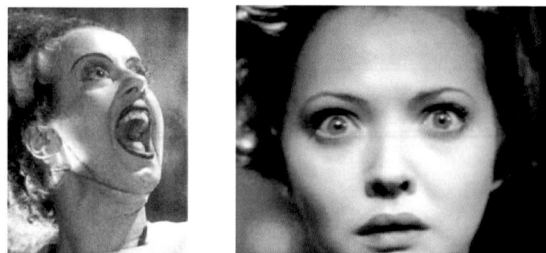

Put expression into Expressionism: Elsa Lanchester, *Bride of Frankenstein*, and Sylvia Sidney, *Fury*.

Beguiling: Mrs Danvers (Judith Anderson) in *Rebecca*, and Norma Desmond (Gloria Swanson). I apologize to Ms. Desmond that the picture got small.

Run scared: Richard Widmark in Jules Dassin's Britpic *Night and the City*.

Hungarian born **MIKLÓS RÓZSA** scored *Sahara* 1943, *Double Indemnity* 1944, and *The Lost Weekend* 1945. Rózsa followed with *The Killers* 1946, *The Strange Love of Martha Ivers* 1946, *Desert Fury* 1947, *The Red House* 1947, *Criss Cross* 1949, and *The Asphalt Jungle* 1950.

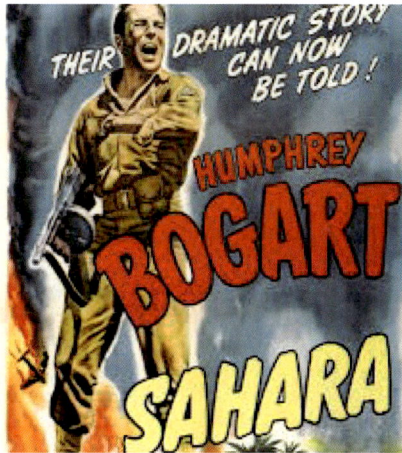

Q. Who might the stern Charles McGraw and William Conrad be in a movie titled *The Killers*?

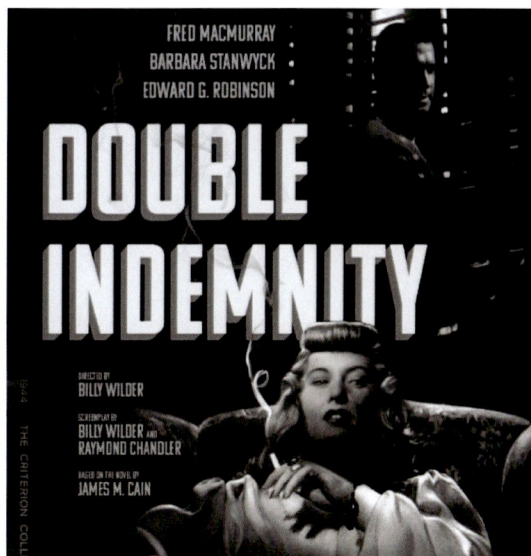

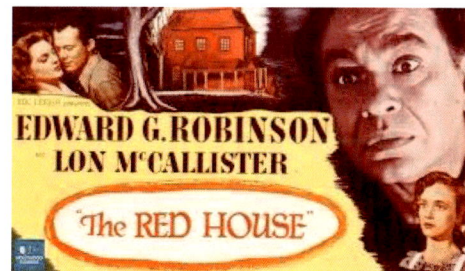

Russian born composer **DIMITRI TIOMKIN** scored across genres and was noted for his Westerns (two Oscars for *High Noon* 1952). Tiomkin scored noirs, including *When Strangers Marry* 1944, *Dillinger* 1945, *The Dark Mirror* 1946, *Whistle Stop* 1946, *Champion* 1949, *D.O.A.* 1950, *The Well* 1951, *I Confess* 1953, and *Dial M for Murder* 1954.

Ava nice night, George? Ava Gardner and George Raft in *Whistle Stop*.

Hunted: Kim Hunter in *When Strangers Marry*.

Two sides: Lawrence Tierney is *Dillinger* and Montgomery Clift is a conflicted priest in *I Confess*.

Seeing double: Olivia de Havilland and Olivia de Havilland star in *The Dark Mirror*.

Noir lover's revenge: I decolorized *Dial M for Murder*, made **in** WarnerColor. Robert Cummings holds an unglamorous Grace Kelly.

Art directors/ set designers

HANS DREIER was an art director in native Germany before moving to the U.S. at the urgings of German director Ernst Lubitsch.

Dreier was Paramount senior art director from 1927-50. He designed the proto-noir Shanghai Express 1932, directed by Josef von Sternberg.

Lily Marlene: Dietrich, pictured with Clive Brook, plays Lily in *Shanghai Express*.

In German Expressionism, sets reflect inner turmoil. Dreir's other noirs include *Double Indemnity* 1944, *The Lost Weekend* 1955, and *Sunset Boulevard*. He won an Oscar for *Samson and Delilah* 1955.

Odds stacked against them: This evocative set in *Double Indemnity* reflects the recklessness of the plan of Barbara Stanwyck and Fred MacMurray.

Homely terror: Ordinary objects menace Ray Milland in *The Lost Weekend*.

Lights, camera, inaction: The set of *Sunset Boulevard* and the actors are arranged to express the grand delusions of former silent-movie star, Norma Desmond (Gloria Swanson).

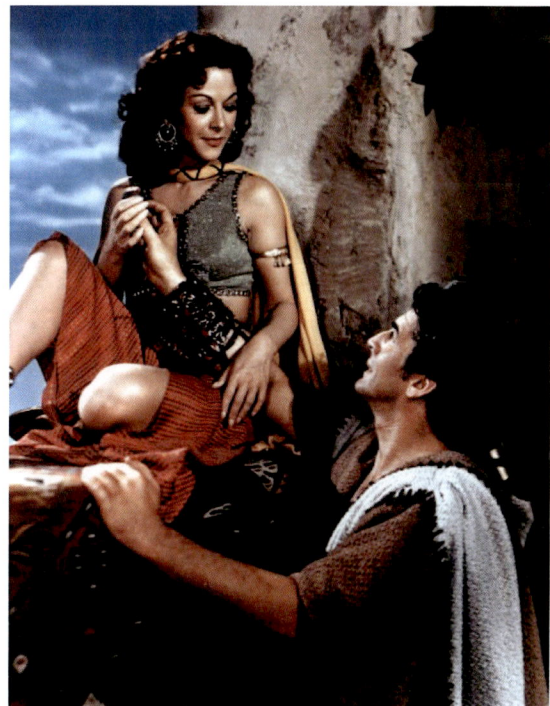

Beware, Sam: Samson (Victor Mature) has Delilah (Hedy Lamarr) on a pedestal but the askew god between them sends a silent warning.

Russian **ALEXANDER GOLITZEN** was art director on *Scarlet Street 1945*. Golitzen was art director *on The Tattered Dress* 1957, and *A Touch of Evil* 1958.

Weird awaits: The strange art décor of Joan Bennett's apartment portends tragedy in her relationship with amateur painter Edward G Robinson in *Scarlet Street*.

Noir motifs: Vertical lines, an askew wall and painting, and shadows around the hands show Jeanne Crain is unable to comfort Jeff Chandler in *The Tattered Dres*s.

Shapely: Spirals and shadows surround the obese Orson Welles in *A Touch of Evil*.

HARRY HORNER born in Bohemia was a set designer and director. He designed the noir *Outrage* 1950 and the neo-noirs *The Hustler* 1961 and *The Driver* 1978.

Turmoil: The grid of a bedhead is a noir favorite to express being in an inner prison of psychological stress. The doll, hanging from the rail at an askew angle in *Outrage*, is a deft touch. Mala Powers plays a rape victim.

Symbolism: Designer Horner surrounds pool shark Paul Newman with symbols in *The Hustler*. The Christian crucifixion is to our right, the boxer's feet above his head, pool "spears" to our left.

Refuge: *The Driver*, Ryan O'Neill, leaves a decaying world to the only place where he is in control.

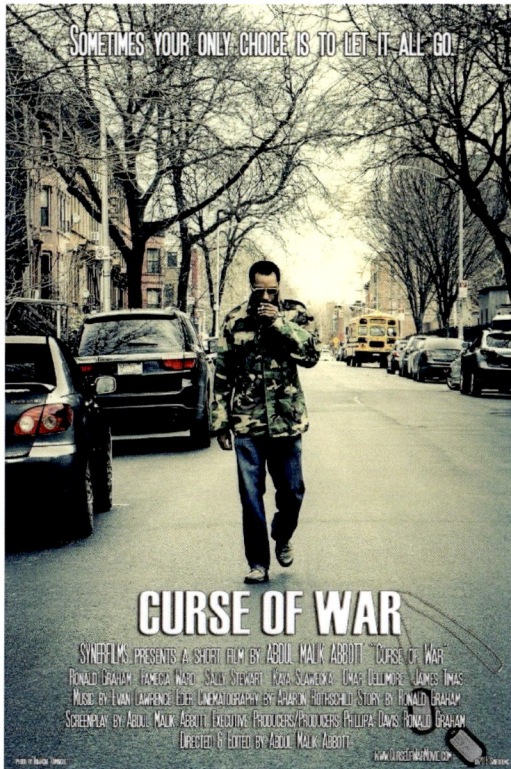

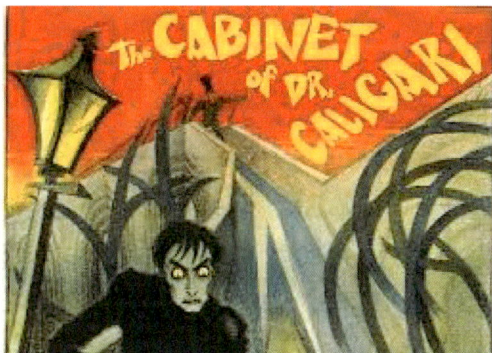

The theme of the 2016 short film *Curse of War* is evident from its title. An ex-marine, returned from service in the Middle East, is drowning the curse in alcohol, and he loses his civilian job and his family. The film concludes with statistics of the high incidence of PTSD among veterans but it does not cite the studies. A 2024 survey found that 29% of Iraq veterans under VA health care had PTSD, the curse of war, after service.

Defeated and demoralized Germans and Austrians were cursed after WWI. To explore curses Expressionists chose horror often imbued with intellectual and artistic perspectives.

The Great Depression of 1929 arrived at the same time as the initial exodus from Europe of Expressionist directors, actors, such as Bela Lugosi, crew, and musicians.

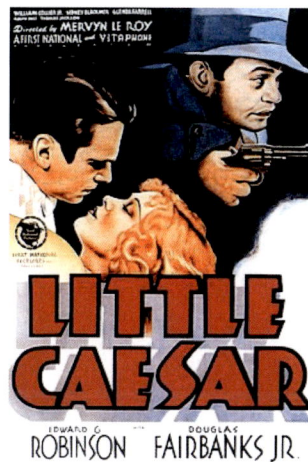

1931

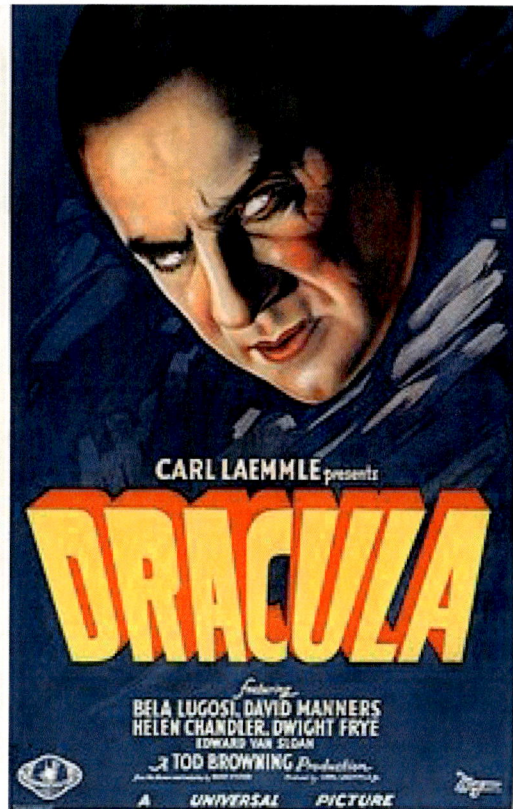

1920

At the same time, Expressionists and the public developed a fondness for the equally bleak gangster movies. *Little Caesar* had a Romanian in the lead, was shot by a Hungarian, and scored by an Italian. Thus were the seedlings of noir.

The answer to why film noir did not emerge as a genre until the 1940s is retrospectivity.

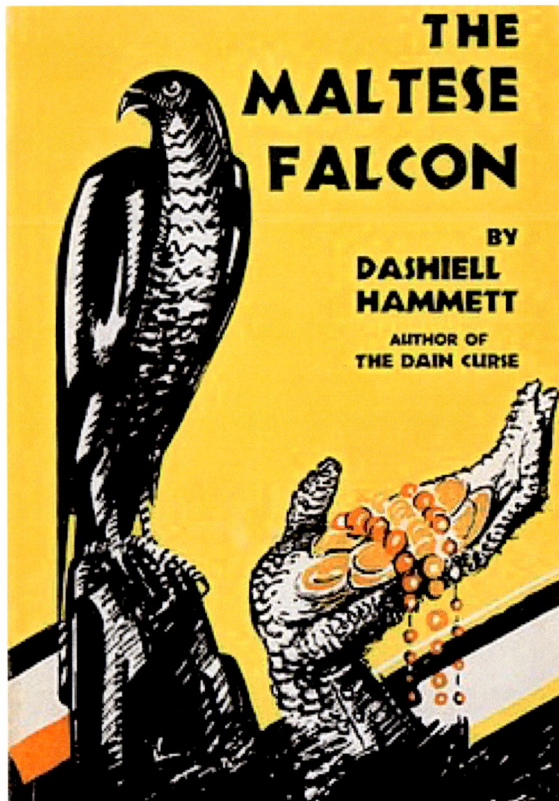

Retrospectivity #1

Alfred A. Knopf published the novel *The Maltese Falcon* in 1930. Warners bought the film rights and made two versions *The Maltese Falcon* 1931, and *Satan Met a Lady* 1936. Neither got the balance of comedy and crime thrills right.

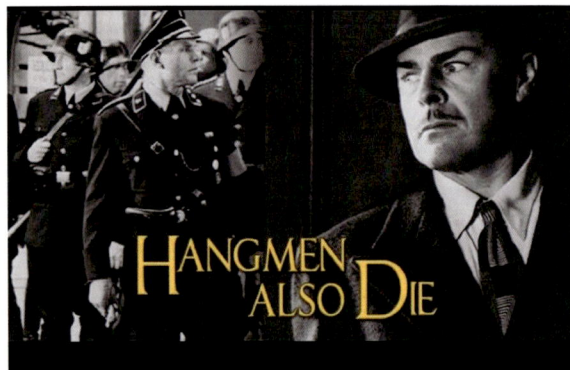

1943

Retrospectivity #2

A genre born out of the first world war and enhanced by the Great Depression, waited until WWII to be reborn as a mutation.

Retrospectivity #3

It always helps discussions to run smoothly when you are talking about the same thing. French film critic Nino Frank, above, discussed four American films from 1941 to 1944 that were only available in France after the war that ended in 1945. Frank must have missed *Stranger on the Third Floor* 1940 or he would have been tempted to include that one.

Frank called the new *kind* (French-word genre) of movies "film noir" (dark film). As these four films were similar, time passed before people shouted at Frank, "It's not a genre."

The films were:

To this day, the four films are regarded as noir classics. Bien choisi, Monsieur Frank.

1955

Cinema is a retrospective artform. Hollywood's appetite for juvenile-delinquency movies sharpened during the mid to late 1950s. There was a juvenile delinquency "problem" in the U.S during World War II, but it ended after the war. It did not "burn" in the 1950s. (Latzer, B. *The Rise and Fall of Violent Crime in America*, Encounter Books, pp. 20-22, p. 70). What Hollywood responded to were political and media beat-ups of this "burning problem".

Which war? Similarly, we should resist casual understanding of film noir's link to WWII. The United States entered the war in December 1941. It was a year later in November 1942 that U.S. troops first saw action overseas. The Falcon flew into cinemas in October 1941, as Warner's third filming of a 1930 novel, written by a WWI veteran.

This timeline explains why the rattle of this simple man plays the tune that sings film noir had its genesis in a world war – the Great War, the War to End All Wars, World War I.

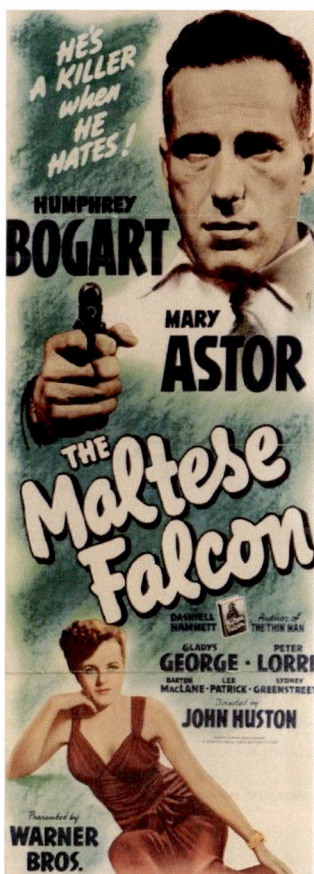

My six pictorial reviews

1944   *Curse*   **1947**

1938   *Crime*   **1955**

1956   *Cringe*   **1946**

1944

Synopsis: rich ugly old man seduces beautiful young women and then destroys them – what relevance would such a storyline have for Hollywood? Well, the producers of *Bluebeard* 1944 felt this French folk tale might make a handy little parable for the movie-going masses.

Being Hollywood, one part of the Bluebeard legend had to be changed – an ugly central character just would not do. Instead, we have the compelling rather than handsome visage of John Carradine, the patriarch of an acting clan with the most prominent member being his son David.

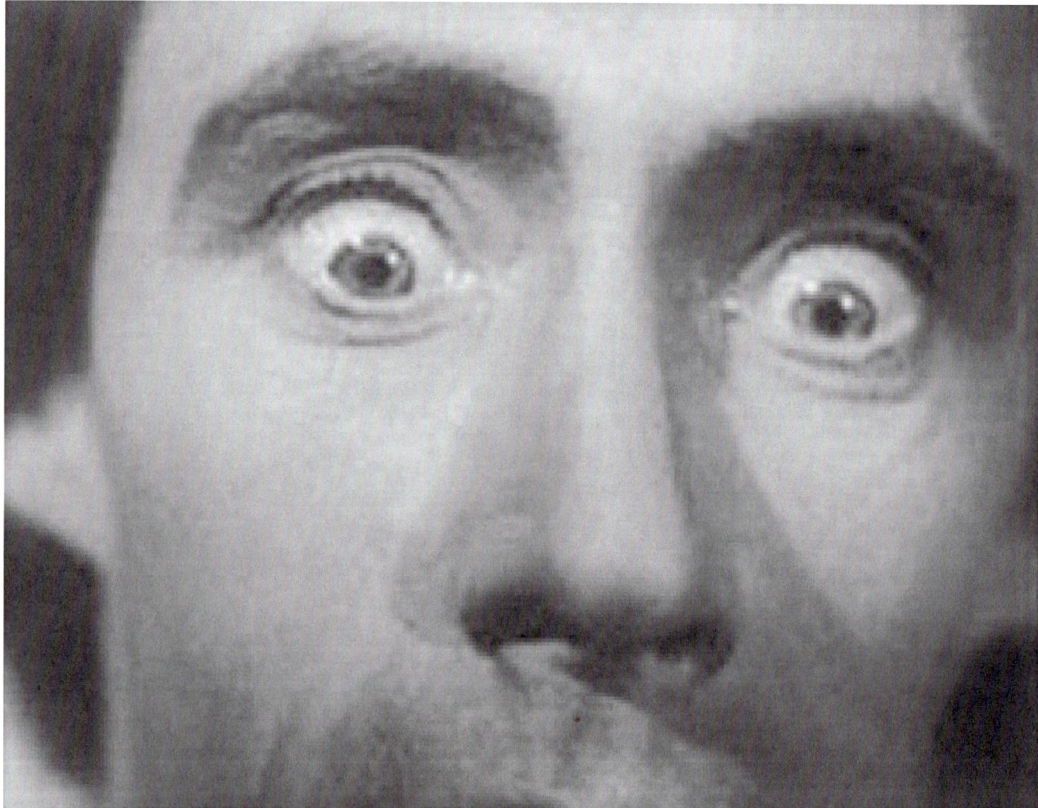

Another change renders the victims from being Bluebeard's wives to models of the painter, come puppeteer, come strange dude.

Some dispute that *Bluebeard* is noir. They say it is a period horror film. But Director Edgar G. Ulmer's distinctive set designs, close-ups, unusual angles, and playing with light and shade make this a noir and one that is underrated.

When I first saw *Bluebeard*, the quality of the print left something to be desired. However, quality of the story and the suspense and the darkness of the theme all combined to make *Bluebeard* eminently watchable.

In 2020, Paramount did a 4k scan restoration which failed to eliminate all the imperfections of the extant prints.

In 2024 Kino Lorber sourced the Paramount restoration for an 80th anniversary Blu-ray version for Region A (North America, South America, U.S. Territories, Japan, South Korea, Taiwan). A bonus feature is a range of old-time horror and sci-fi trailers including Ulmer's *The Man from Planet X* 1951.

I don't do product placement, but I make an exception here as an unpaid public service. My country of Australia is not in Region A, so no quid pro quo.

The studio

PRODUCERS RELEASING CORPORATION (PRC) was a Hollywood film studio and distribution house in what was called Poverty Row, a term originally applied to a stretch of Gower Street in Hollywood known for low-budget studios. Rents were cheap. Over time, Poverty Row stood for any less-salubrious Hollywood addresses where B-movies were created.

Intersecting with North Gower St. was Sunset Boulevard (of broken dreams?). Even the title of Billy Wilder's 1950 noir satire was a joke.

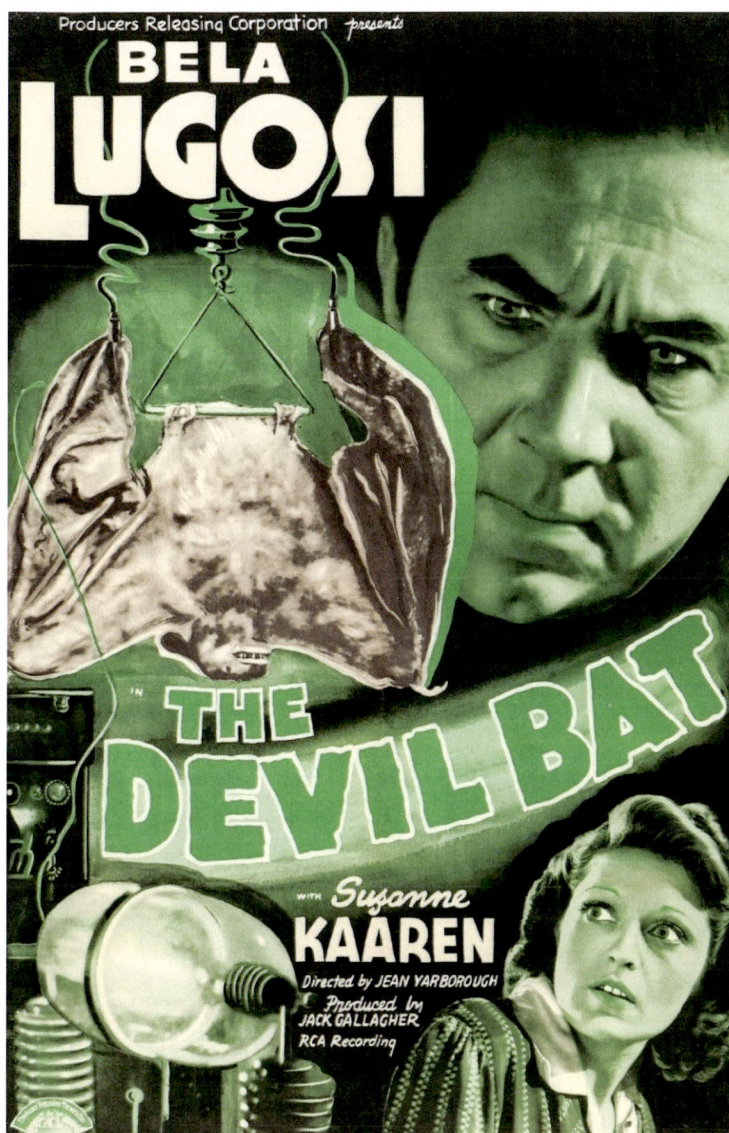

PRC lasted from 1939-47. The studio had an early success with *The Devil Bat* 1940 starring Bela "Dracula" Lugosi. The director Jean Yarbrough went on to popular comedy franchises, Abbott and Costello, and the Bowery Boys.

Later in life, Suzanne Kaaren from *The Devil Bat* played a five-year role as one of NY rent-controlled tenants who overcame Donald Trump in the 1980s. Trump owned the old residential building at 100 Central Park South in which Kaaren lived. Trump wanted to turn it into luxury condominiums, but he failed at law to evict the tenants. They claimed Trump cut heat and hot water, and demanded they undo renovations allowed by the previous owner of the building (Pagliery, J. *Donald Trump was a nightmare landlord in the 1980s*, CNN Money 2016).

By 1986, Trump had spent more than $1 million fighting the tenants and had spent only $160,000 in repairs over the previous four years, according to statements filed by his legal team. Trump settled with the counter-suing tenants' association in 1986. He reimbursed $550,000 for their legal fees and agreed to let the housing agency monitor repairs for five years.

The 1942 war movie *A Yank in Libya* showed film viewers' taste for patriotic exotic adventures achieved by PRC's respect for low-budget accuracy-averse tales. Comic relief was Parkyakarkus, a pseudonym of Harry Einstein. Being of Russian and Austrian origin, following Hollywood tradition, he popularized the Greek Chef Nick Parkyakarkus, a persona he took to radio and film.

Like father like sons: Harry Einstein was the father of comedians Albert Brooks, centre, and the late Bob Einstein.

In *A Yank in Libya*, Romanian-born Duncan Renaldo plays Shiek David and Mexican-born George J. Lewis plays Shiek Ibrahim.

The cinematographer was Eddie Linden who shot *King Kong* 1933.

In 1943, Robert Young, owner of Pathé Industries film processing, acquired the studio. Films received higher budgets, though well below second-string films of the majors. Films featured an amended logo, above.

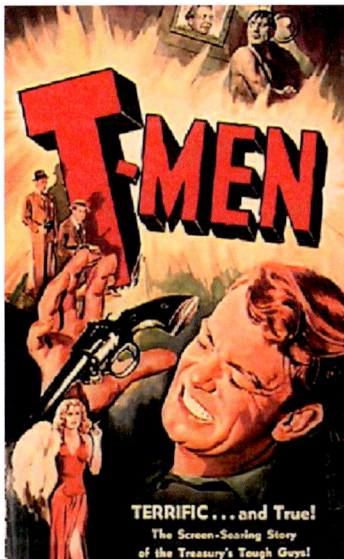

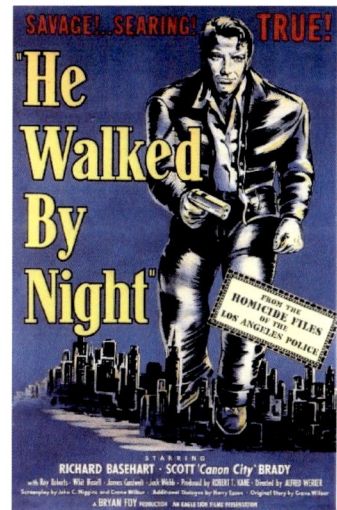

Pathé established Eagle-Lion Films to swallow up PRC in 1947. Legendary names of film noir were part of the short-lived Eagle-Lion – producers Edward Small and Walter Wanger, cinematographer John Alton, director Anthony Mann, actors Claire Trevor and Dennis O'Keefe. The studio produced the noir classics *T-Men* 1947, *Raw Deal* 1948, and *He Walked by Night* 1948.

Unfortunately, fiscal management was not as productive as the low-budget movies. Eagle-Lion closed the studio in November 1948.

Noir misses: Edgar Ulmer's early PRC films did not shine. But attractive set designs and strong visuals were signs that higher budgets were all that were needed. *Tomorrow We Live* 1942, centre, and *Girls in Chains* 1943 preceded *Bluebeard*.

Austrian-born and raised set designer turned director Edgar G. Ulmer began working for PRC in 1942 and was there in time to take advantage of the better budgets. He directed three films in rapid succession: *Bluebeard* 1944, *Strange Illusion* 1945 and *Detour* 1945. *Strange Illusion* was beneath the standards of the other two, which I regard as noir classics.

Kill the one you love over and over: John Carradine and Sonia Sorel who plays a good bit part here and in *Strange Illusion*. Carradine and Sorel wed in 1945. She was the mother of actors Keith and Robert Carradine. Actors David and Bruce were the son of Carradine's first wife, Ardanelle McCool. Actor Michael Bowen Jr. is the son of Sorel and 1960s counter-cultural visual artist Michael Bowen who organised the 1967 Flower Power anti-war protest outside the Pentagon.

Ulmer who was busted from the major studios for dalliance with the wrong woman always remembered he was working in the exploitative Bs. The first corpse dragged from the Seine has her dress caught in her underwear. Carradine walks in on three women, one in her underwear. The prurience was subtle and did not linger. Ulmer was a serious filmmaker.

It takes a while to get there but the theme of Bluebeard is the danger of men who idealize women, put them on a pedestal, as they used to say, back in the day. Visual artist Gaston Morrell (Carradine) is haunted by the memory of the "Maid of Orleans" he painted turning out to be a prostitute (and, in a bit of side nonsense from Ulmer, one who participates in threesomes). The consequences are deadly, unleashing another homme fatal on the loose.

JOHN CARRADINE played in more than 300 films, mostly B-pictures. He is excellent as gaunt tormented Bluebeard, a scary nemesis but with a dash of redemptive pitiable sorrow.

John Carradine's warm voice renders his character of the seductive serial killer believable.

Before *Bluebeard* Carradine had a significant bit part in the good 1941 noir *Swamp Water*.

He was male lead as a real-life Nazi in the exquisitely titled *Hitler's Madman* 1943. It was originally called *Hitler's Hangman,* changed to avoid confusion with Fritz Lang's *Hangmen Also Die.* Director Douglas Sirk made *Hitler's Madman* at PRC in a week.

After *Bluebear*d, Carradine did a great support role in the noir *Fallen Angel* 1945. He plays fake spiritualist Professor Madley. *Fallen Angel,* directed by Otto Preminger, is a much underrated noir, as good as Preminger's *Laura* 1944.

TEALA LORING is undercover police agent Francine Lutien, the sister of Lucille (played by female lead Jean Parker).

Loring had a busy 1944 in the Bs. She also managed to score an uncredited role as a telephone operator in the higher-budget noir classic *Double Indemnity* 1944. Poverty Row was a good address for better parts in (financially) worse pictures.

T 'n T: Tod Andrews and Teala Loring in a publicity shot for *Return of the Ape Man* 1944.

Female lead Loring's name was not on the men-only poster for *Return of the Ape Man*. She was in the cast under the name Judith Gibson, and Tod Andrews was billed as Michael Ames. Andrews began his career as Ames and Loring was on loan from Paramount, where she was Gibson before her name change.

Loring's other films of 1944 were *Delinquent Daughters* (outstandingly bad), and *Sweethearts of the U.S.A.*

She was uncredited for *I love a Soldier*, *Henry Aldrich's Little Secret*, and *Standing Room Only*.

Loring gave the acting game away in 1950.

The Player

JEAN PARKER appeared in 70 movies from 1932 to 1966 as well as being a successful businesswoman and enduring four marriages.

Parker entered the folklore of my country Australia in 1951. A swimsuit inspector measured her bikini and declared it skimpy and kicked her off Sydney's Bondi Beach .

The story made the international press and, back in Hollywood, Chief Censor Joe Breen would have been proud of Aussie Beach Inspector Abe Laidlaw, protecting Australian morals with his tape measure.

Parker's film career was off to a promising start with good roles at 17 in Frank Capra's sentimental comedy *Lady for A Day* and George Cukor's *Little Women*, both 1933. But she progressed into B-movies, and she diversified into theatre and coaching acting. She starred in the noirs *Dead Man's Eyes* 1944 with Lon Chaney Jr., directed by Reginald Le Borg, and *Black Tuesday* 1954, directed by Argentinian Hugo Fregonese.

Inspector Bill Willis told Miss Parker, when she took off her white robe, "You must leave at once.

"You are making an exhibition of yourself. Please go," he said.

Miss Parker argued she thought the costume would be allowed here, but Willis remained firm and escorted her to the promenade, where she entered a waiting car.

Her husband, actor Robert Lowery, was with her all the time, and smiling, stood back silently while the inspector was present.

"Publicity"

A beach inspector said later he believed Miss Parker was posing for publicity pictures, as a photographer was present before she arrived.

He went on the beach with her, and later drove her away in his car.

Beach Inspector Aub. Laidlaw said later the costume was "below all decency."

Miss Parker said later, "I have never been so embarrassed in all my life.

"I went down to try out your famous Bondi and as soon as I took off my coat and started to comb my hair the beach inspector came up and told me to leave.

"I have worn this swimsuit in California and several places without complaint."

Miss Parker produced from a pocket two pieces of flimsy green material, white-spotted, which she

Shocked: Jean Parker shocks an Aussie Inspector with a tape measure in one hand.
Media report: The Sun newspaper, Sydney, Fri 2 Nov 1951.

NILS ASTHER plays Inspector Jacques Lefevre in *Bluebeard*.

Asther was a Danish-born Swedish actor active in Hollywood from 1926.

Described as impossibly handsome and the male Garbo, Asther made 16 films in the silent era, including two with Greta Garbo. Above left is a love scene from *Wild Orchids*, and right is a scene from *The Single Standard*. Both 1929 films were with synchronized sound and were box-office smashes.

Watching: Asther plays an aspiring actor in the Swedish film *The Wings* 1916. Asther is peripheral to the central plot of a heterosexual countess trying to destroy a gay relationship.

Asther was blackballed in 1934 by all major studios for walking out on MGM. Other factors worked against him. Studios deemed his overt homosexuality bad for PR, and his Swedish accent an impediment for talkies. Most telling was that Asther was a vocal critic of the studio system by which studios owned stars. Asther was forced to leave Hollywood in 1935 and stay away until 1940.

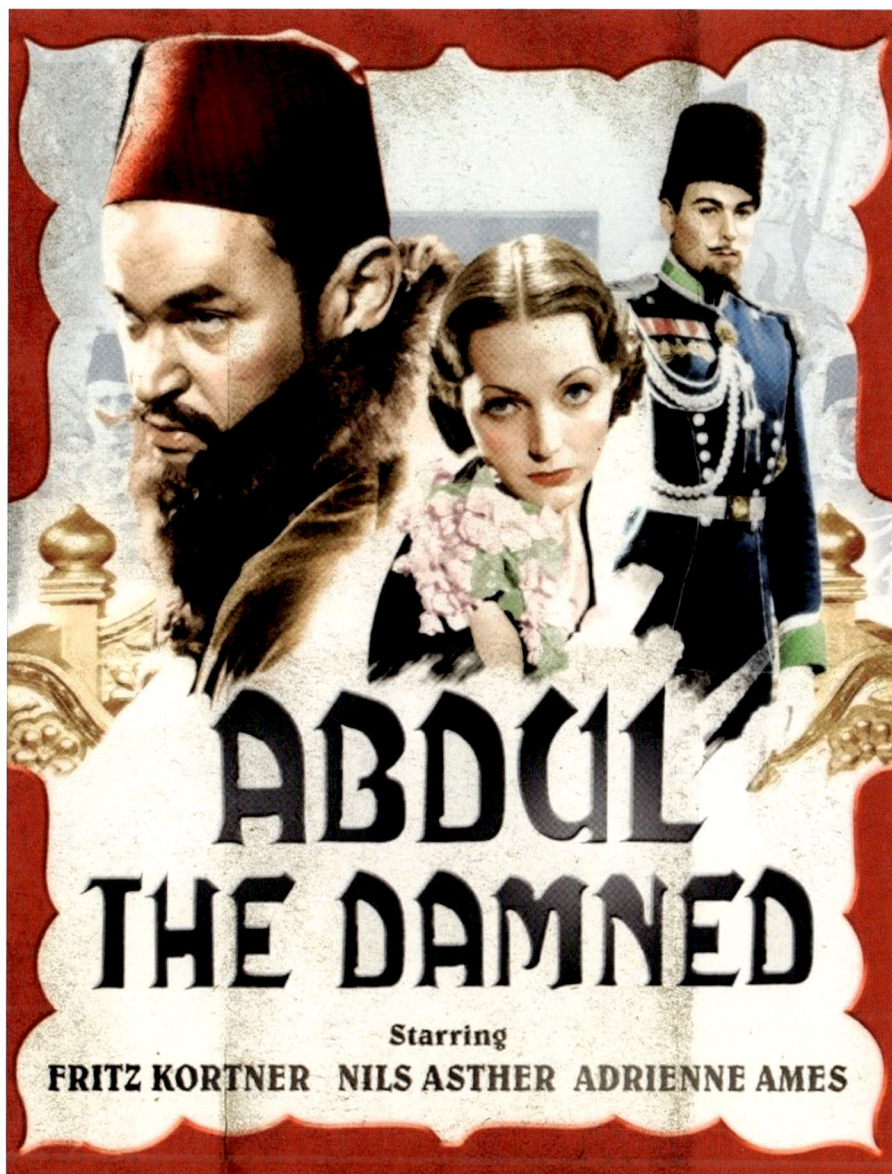

The most intriguing of Asther's British films of his exile was based on a true story of the Young Turks deposing the Ottoman Sultan Abdul Hamid II in 1908-9. In *Abdul the Damned* 1935, Asther plays the mythical Chief of Police Kadar-Pasha who murders to keep the Sultan in power.

Austrian Fritz Kortner who played Abdul was a respected stage and screen actor who played the lead in the German drama *Dreyfus* 1930, an account of the infamous anti-Semitic injustice in France from 1894-1906. Fleeing the rise of Hitler, Kortner made films in Britain and America. A pioneer of German Expressionism, Kortner appeared in the 1947 Hollywood film noir *The Brasher Doubloon*, based on Raymond Chandler's novel *The High Window* 1942.

Critics vary on *The Brasher Doubloon*'s value. The banter between leads George Montgomery and Nancy Guild is forced. Monty is more sleazy than witty. Veterans Florence Bates and Kortner are good.

1941   1941   1942

Back in Hollywood, Asther immersed himself in support roles in low-budget movies, hoping to recapture success that never arrived.

Of interest is *The Night Before the Divorce*, a comedy involving three people who would leave their mark on noir that decade – director Robert Siodmak (*The Spiral Staircase* 1945, *The Killers* 1946, *Cry of the City* 1948, *Criss Cross* 1949) and actors Lynn Bari (*Nocturne* 1946, *The Amazing Mr. X* 1948) and Mary Beth Hughes (*The Great Flamarion* 1945).

Asther led the 1945 horror noir *The Man in Half Moon Street*, available in DVD and Blu-ray worldwide.

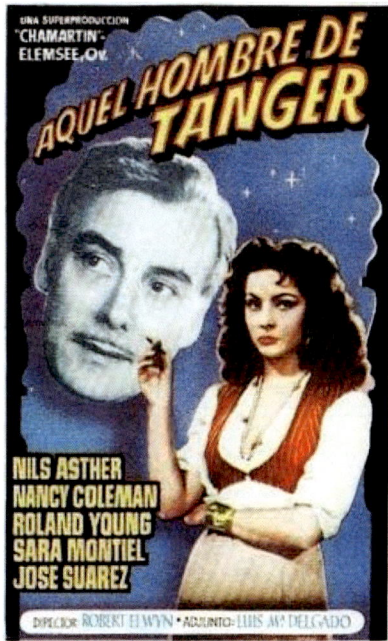

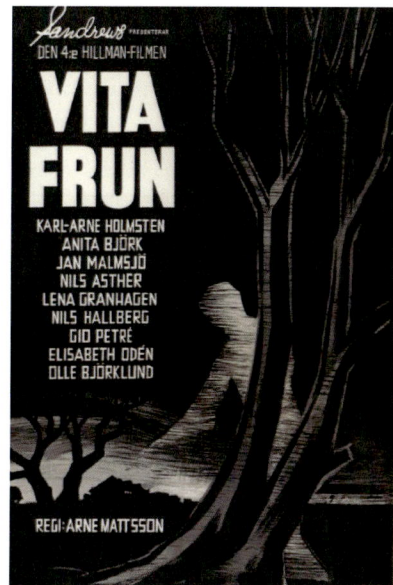

Asther had to return to Europe for leads in the Spanish-American *That Man from Tangier* 1953, the Swedish *When Darkness Falls* 1960, and a prominent role in *The Lady in White* 1962, also from Sweden. Those Swedish filmmakers knew the art of making attractive posters.

The 1963 Danish drama *Suddenly, a Woman!* marked Asther's 47th year in the business. On that note of longevity, he retired.

Aged 84, Asther died in Stockholm in 1981.

The Hays Code of censorship introduced in 1930 was enforced once Joseph Breen became the chief censor in 1934. Filmmakers did not worry much about the code during its early pre-Breen years of 1930-33.

In the first talkies, Nils Asther played people of different nationalities such as a Chinese man in *The Bitter Tea of General Yen* 1932 directed by Frank Capra. The film portrayed miscegenation (inter-racial relations) between the characters played by Asther and future noir icon Barbara Stanwyck. The code forbade the depiction of miscegenation, and same-gender relationships as perversions but, pre-Breen, *The Bitter Tea of General Yen* escaped into the cinemas to lukewarm public reception.

In 1950 when Censor Breen was still in power, Columbia wanted to re-release *The Bitter Tea of General Yen,* feeling the film did not receive the acclaim it deserved first time around. The Hays Office advised against it and the re-release never happened. It is now available in HD or SD to rent or buy.

What would Bluebeard want with me?

The answer better be, "a lot more than nothing" or this movie is going nowhere.

The Verdict *Bluebeard*

★★★★☆

Curse1947

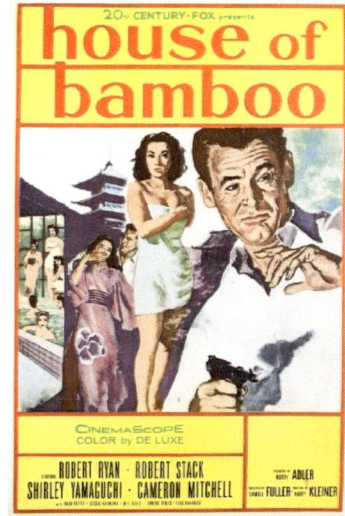

Houses of Noir: Made of rage,   resentment,   and   Asian bamboo.

The horror noir, *The Red House*, sometimes classified as a thriller, is a movie sadly neglected in noir retrospectives. Like Edward G. Robinson's 1949 noir *House of Strangers*, *The Red House* is excluded from best-noir lists.

Both are better movies than four Samuel Fuller films among the well regarded *Slant Magazine 100 best film noirs of all time*. Highly rated Fuller flicks are *Underworld U.S.A.* 1961 at #40, *The Naked Kiss* 1964 at #55 (really!) *The Crimson Kimono* 1959 at #83 and *House of Bamboo* 1955 at #100. You've got the wrong house. It should be the Strangers' or the Red one. Fuller's *Pickup on South Street* 1953 #12 deserves its high spot.

Lust or love: Lon McCallister is torn between the capricious Julie London and the caring Allene Roberts.

43

Bad boy for lust: Rory Calhoun plays hard-to-get with juvenile femme fatale Julie London who was a celebrated singer, remembered for the worldwide hit *Cry Me a River* 1955.

Cleverly plotted, *The Red House* unveils four sets of parallel relationships, the first, a 15-yr old mystery at the core of the film's suspense.

In the second, Julie London is going steady with reliable Lon McCallister, but bad-boy forest-dweller, Rory Calhoun, seduces her.

This mirrors another threesome in which London is the wild one, threatening the growing relationship between McCallister and Allene Roberts.

Another trio has Judith Anderson sacrificing a loving relationship to stay with and calm her brother, stricken with PTSD after the unsuccessfully sublimated horror of 15 years earlier.

It is significant this movie emerged two years after the end of WWII. Veterans would have carried into the cinemas their own PTSD, or combat stress reaction (CSR) as it was then called. The curse of war was on the screen and in the cinema.

Daves

Maltz

The Red House director Delmar Daves wrote the script along with the uncredited Albert Maltz, under investigation by the House Un-American Activities Committee. The HUAC imprisoned, fined, and blacklisted Maltz.

Maltz co-wrote the noir *Naked City* 1948 before two decades of being blacklisted.

Using AI, technicians colorized *The Red House* in 2021. But, in its original monochrome, director Daves and cinematographer Bert Glennon (Oscars for the John Ford Western *Stagecoach* 1939, and the aviation adventure *Dive Bomber* 1941) created perfect contrast of shadowy night and bright day.

The eerie sounds of a theremin create and sustain suspense during the well-lit scenes set in a rural community.

The musical inventor

Committed Russian communist Leon Theremin (1896-1993) invented one of the world's first electronic musical instruments, and it bore his name. A scientist working in the new field of electricity, Theremin built a motion detector that created sounds when his hand accidentally interrupted the magnetic field. The theremin, an instrument the player did not touch, was born.

On a propaganda tour of Europe and the U.S. Theremin demonstrated what he said was inexpensive, easy to play, would reconstruct orchestras and be in every home, taking musicianship to the masses. He convinced radio maker RCA and sold them the U.S. production rights. RCA repeated Theremin's wish that one would be in every home.

The problem was the theremin was not easy to play. Even its inventor was not proficient. And it could not produce a range of melodious sounds. What it could do was produce startlingly eerie sounds. Above, Alexandra Stepanoff rocks it for radio in 1930.

Composer Shostakovich scored the theremin for its first cinematic contribution in the Russian film *Alone* (1931, directed by Leonid Trauberg and Grigori Kozintsev). Trauberg received the 1941 Stalin prize. Authorities castigated him during the post-war Stalinist anti-Semitic campaigns. Fellow Jew Kozintsev avoided censure during the purge that affected his friends and colleagues.

The scene that used the theremin was of a rising snowstorm. History did not record who played the theremin. One source said musicians were averse to the Shostakovich using experimental instruments.
(https://www.classicalsource.com/cd/shostakovich-odna-alone).

It took a while for Hollywood to realize the theremin could have audiences spellbound but astute 1940s creators cottoned on. The first was Alfred Hitchcock. *Spellbound* 1945 musical director Miklós Rózsa scored the theremin played by Dr. Samuel Hoffmann. Rózsa won the Oscar.

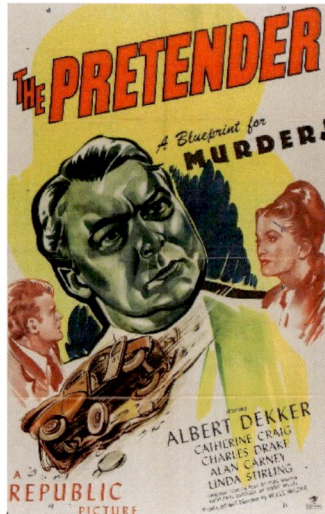

Rózsa and Dr. Hoffmann brought their theremin to the alcoholic noir Billy Wilder's *The Lost Weekend*, also 1945, which was nominated for the music Oscar. Dr. Hoffmann played the instrument for the noirs *The Red House*, *The Pretender* (1947, directed by Billy's brother, W. Lee Wilder) and *Raw Deal* 1948. Rózsa also scored the noir *A Double Life* 1947, a title appropriate for the classical composer whose works graced grand concert halls and whose noirs received second billing at less salubrious cinemas.

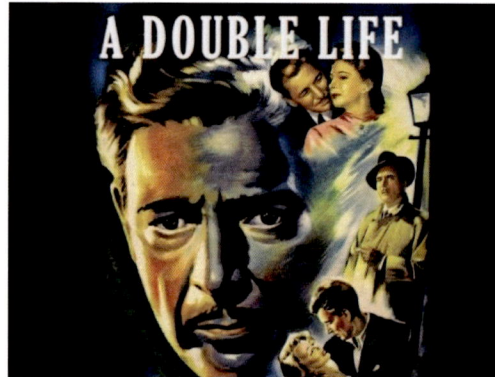

Winners: Miklós Rózsa and lead actor Ronald Colman won Academy Awards for *A Double Life*. It is not one of my favorite noirs. I find the premise of a top theatrical actor possessed by his roles as rather silly.

Miklós Rózsa called his autobiography *A Double Life* (Baton Wicks Publications; 1984).

Frankly, it's portable: Maggie Gyllenhaal never goes anywhere without her theremin in the captivating comedy *Frank* 2014.

Frank is an exceptionally good movie, deviating slightly in the last act from its track to greatness.

Hungarian born **MIKLÓS RÓZSA** contributed to upwards of twenty noirs if you include the stock music he created for film libraries.

William Wyler's multiple Oscar nominated *Detective Story* 1951 used the stock music of Rózsa and Victor Young (22-times Oscar nominated, winning once, posthumously for *Around the World in 80 Days* 1957. Young was not noted for noirs though he scored the excellent noir Western *Johnny Guitar* 1954).

Notable noirs to use Rózsa stock were *Johnny Stool Pigeon* 1949, *Border Incident* 1949, *Woman In Hiding* 1950, *The Asphalt Jungle* 1950, *Someone Up There Likes Me* 1957, Egyptian noir *Cairo Station* 1958, and *The Trap* 1959.

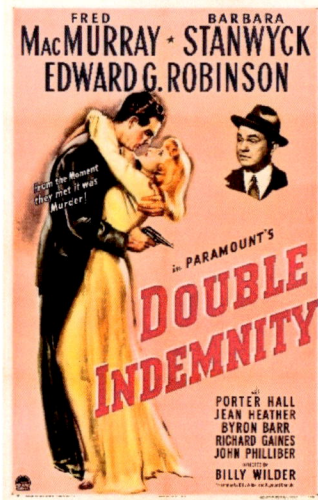

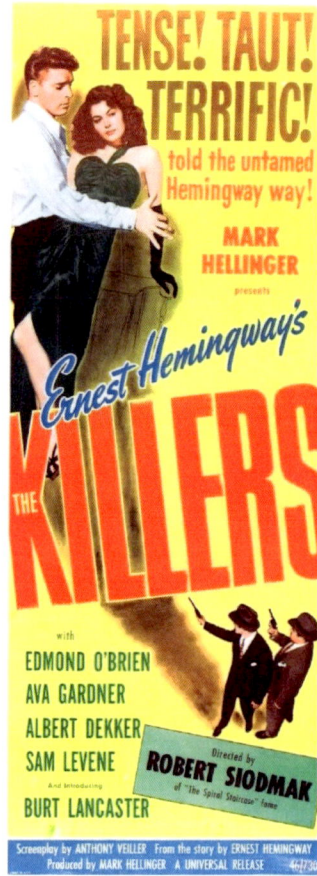

Celebrated noirs Miklós Rózsa received credit and acclaim for were *Double Indemnity* 1944, *The Killers* 1946, *Brute Force* 1947, and *Naked City* 1948.

JUDITH ANDERSON is immortalized from her role as the sinister housekeeper Mrs. Danvers in Alfred Hitchcock's gothic thriller *Rebecca* 1940. Anderson, an Australian who had endured poverty in her U.S. career during World War I, worked her way up to be a theatrical star of the 1930s.

She played Lady Macbeth opposite Laurence Olivier at the Old Vic, London, in 1937. She might have been inspired to transfer that role to Mrs. Danvers.

Rebecca gave her a triumphant return to film after she had few roles earlier. Anderson received an Academy Award nomination for best support.

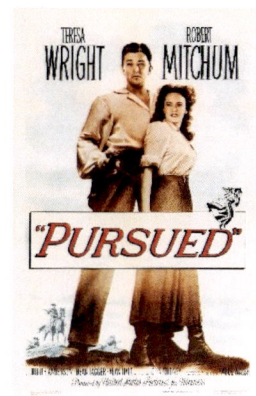

Anderson's noirs before *The Red House* were *Lady Scarface* 1941 followed by the classics *Laura* 1944 and *The Strange Love of Martha* Ivers 1946, and the noir Western *Pursued* 1947, directed by Raoul Walsh and shot by James Wong Howe. Martin Scorsese contributed to the restoration of *Pursued*.

Emmanuel Goldenberg was born in Bucharest, Romania, in 1893. He was 10-years-old when he came with his family to the United States. In 1913, Emmanuel started acting and changed his name.

The G. in **EDWARD G, ROBINSON** stood for his family name Goldenberg. His friends and family called him Manny. In this way, he always remained Emmanuel Goldenberg.

Manny spent 15 years in stock theatre with only two forays into film when he decided silent pictures shot out of chronological order were not for him. Robinson decided to try his hand at the new talkies, He was fortunate to team up for a 1929 film with future noir director Robert Florey (*The Face Behind the Mask* 1941, *The Crooked Way* 1949) and cinematographer George Joseph Folsey (*The Man with a Cloak* 1951, the noir sci-fi *The Forbidden Planet* 1957).

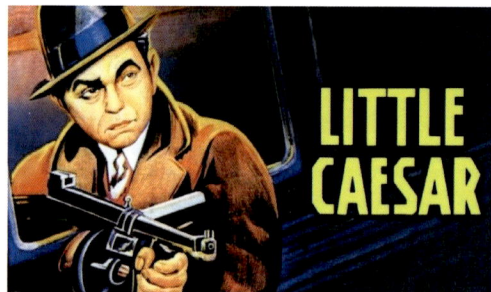

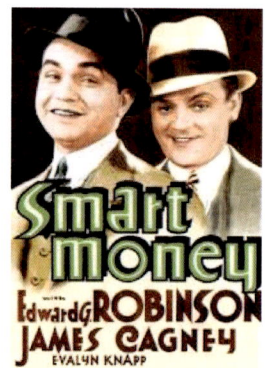

The Florey film was *The Hole in the Wall* and Robinson starred beside another theatrical actor Claudette Colbert. Other gangster movies that followed included *Little Caesar* 1930 which made Robinson a star. In *Smart Money* 1931, he partnered with that other favorite gangster James "Jimmy" Cagney. This was the only time they worked together. Both Robinson and Cagney made movies with Humphrey Bogart. There was no animosity among the trio.

One of Robinson's weirdest movies, by today's standards, was *The Hatchet Man* 1932. It was set in Chinatown, San Francisco, beginning with the World War I Tong wars. Robinson played Wong Low Get. Loretta Young was Sun Toya San, and J. Carrol Naish (of Irish extraction) played Sun Yat Ming.

Being pre-Hays Code enforcement, it is quite a lusty tale of revenge, adultery, and Honor. *The Hatchet Man*, Buddha's avenging angel, performed solidly at the box office, grossing almost three times its budget.

Glad and Manny: Jean Arthur was born Gladys Greene.

Robinson trod water in his career until along came the comedy *The Whole Town's Talking* 1935, based on a story by W.R. Burnett (*Little Caesar*, *High Sierra* 1941) and directed by John Ford (*The Informer* 1935, *Stagecoach* 1939, *The Grapes of Wrath* 1940). Cinematographer Joseph August (*The Informer*, *Gunga Din* 1939, *The Hunchback of Notre Dame* 1939, and *Portrait of Jennie* 1948) was co-founder of the American Society of Cinematographers (ASC).

The Whole Town's Talking boosted the stop-start Hollywood career of Jean Arthur, 34, who went on to be a star of the late 1930s (*The Plainsman* 1936 and *Mr. Smith Goes to Washington* 1939) and early 1940s until her retirement in 1944. She returned for the Western *Shane* 1953.

The Whole Town's Talking made fun of Robinson's cigar-chomping gangster persona.

The cinematographer, August, captured some proto-noir designs as well as fancy quasi art-house shots that matched the snappy dialogue and appealing acting of the two-leads (three if you count Robinson's dual roles. Classic Hollywood loved doppelgangers).

Even small touches such as staid Robinson identifying himself as Arthur Ferguson Jones were winners.

★★★★☆

Robinson's best movie over the next years was the boxing proto-noir *Kid Galahad 1937* with a top performance by Bette Davis, stricken by unrequired love for Wayne Morris. As they often did in the second half of the 1930s, Warner Brothers cast Humphrey Bogart as a villainous gangster. Michael Curtiz directed.

Robinson, an anti-fascist, starred in the first antifa film *Confessions of a Nazi Spy 1939* produced before Europe was engulfed in World War II.

Hays Office censors headed by Joseph Breen wanted the film pulled. In my previous volume on rebels and censors I discussed whether Breen was a bigot and anti-Semite. The Hays Office or Production Code Administration, PCA, said it was unfair to vilify Hitler "considering his phenomenal public career, his unchallenged political and social achievements." (Maddow, Rachel, *Prequel: An American Fight Against Fascism* p. 144, *Transworld* eBook)

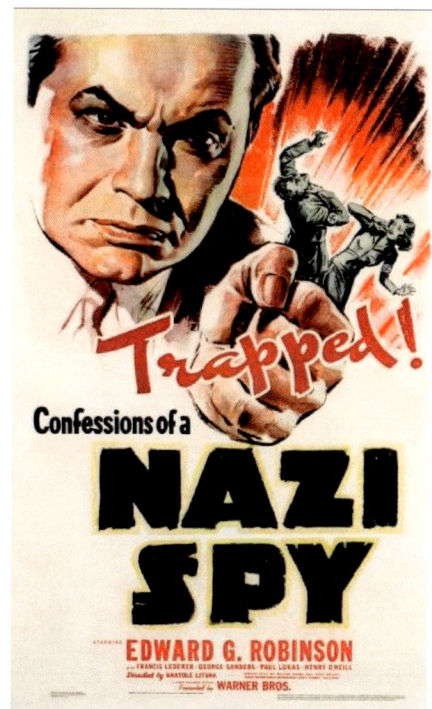

Producer Warners overcame the objections of the PCA and the fledging House Unamerican Activities Committee. The HUAC had a long memory and graylisted (unofficially blacklisted) Robinson from 1950-53. Confessions director Anatole Litvak (*Sorry Wrong Number* 1948), anticipating a blacklisting, left Hollywood in 1952 to spend the rest of his days in Europe, dying in Paris in 1974.

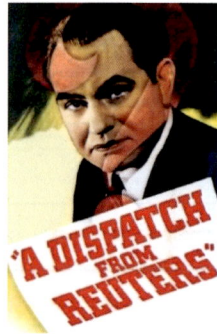

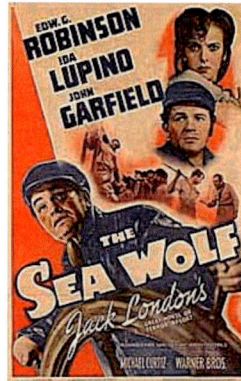

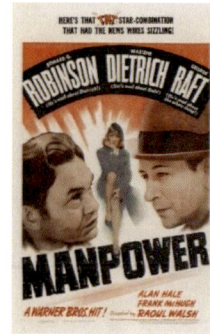

In 1940, Robinson scored with another gangster comedy *Brother Orchid* with comedian Ann Sothern and Warner lightweight heavy, Bogart. *A Despatch from Reuters* 1940 was an entertaining biopic about the man who started the news agency. The nautical adventure drama *The Sea Wolf* 1940 featured three actors who would become icons of film noir. The tagline of *Manpower* – *That TNT star combination that had the news wires sizzling* – sounds cryptic to us today. It referred to a physical fight between Robinson and Raft that a *Life* magazine photographer captured. As well as a top director in Raoul Walsh and three strong leads in the crime drama, the supporting cast included Frank McHugh, Eve Arden, Alan Hale, Barton MacLane, Ward Bond, and Walter Catlett.

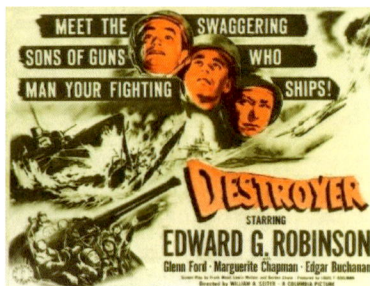

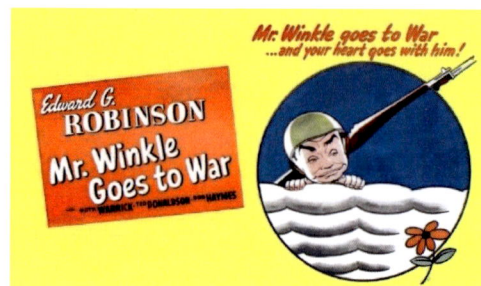

Robinson's war-time movies included *Destroyer* 1943. The protagonist was a shipyard worker and WWI veteran who pulled strings to enlist for the crew of the titular ship. The scenario emulated real-life but Robinson, 48-years-old, was rejected for war service.

The female lead in *Tampico* 1944 Lynn Bari played a femme fatale in two 1946 noirs, *Shock* and *Nocturne*.

Joan Harrison produced *Nocturne* and other noirs *Phantom Lady* 1944, *The Strange Affair of Uncle Harry* 1945, *Ride the Pink Horse* 1947, and *They Won't Believe Me* 1947. Virginia Van Upp (*Gilda* 1946) and Harriet Parsons (*Clash by Night* 1952) were the only other women producing in Hollywood about this time.

Robinson's character in the *Mr Winkle Goes to War* 1944 is drafted at 44. The film was accurate. Defense took men aged 18-45, but fit men to 60 had to register.

Between 1945 and 1949 Robinson starred in seven films that are in the lexicon of film noir or, at least, in my version of the lexicon. They are on the pages following.

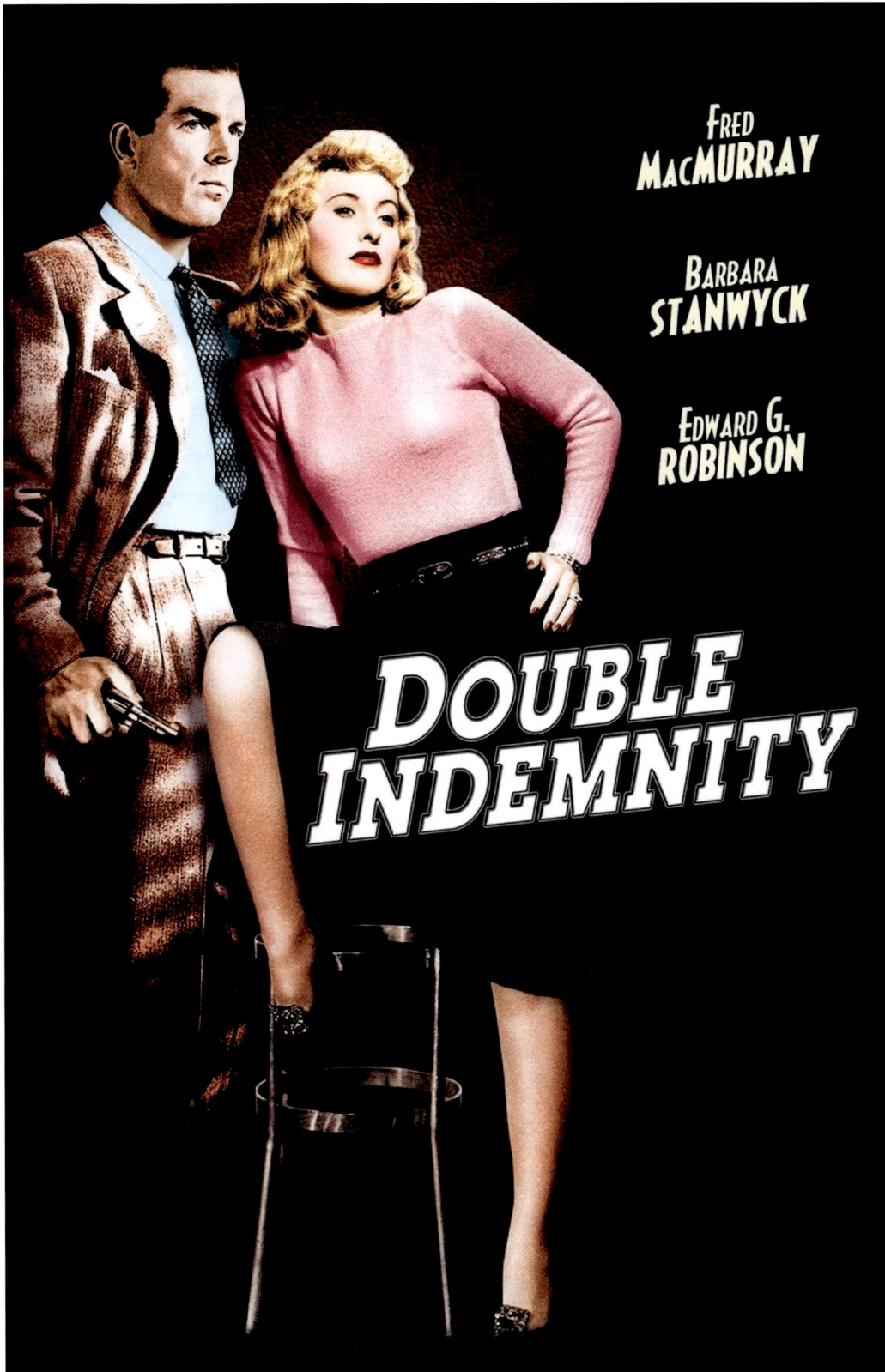

FRED MacMURRAY

BARBARA STANWYCK

EDWARD G. ROBINSON

DOUBLE INDEMNITY

1944

A too-beautiful woman, a too-carefree man—and an evening of gay flirtation shifting madly into a panic of guilt and fear and crimson MURDER ...

...THAT'S EXCITEMENT FOR YOU!

International Pictures, Inc. Presents

EDWARD G. ROBINSON
and
JOAN BENNETT

The Woman in the Window

IT'S THE SCREEN'S SUPREME ADVEN-TURE IN SUSPENSE!

with
RAYMOND MASSEY
and
Edmond Breon · Dan Duryea

Directed by FRITZ LANG
A NUNNALLY JOHNSON Production
Released by RKO RADIO PICTURES, Inc.

1944

Don't let your imagination run wild over "gay flirtation"
but
Do add importance to the villainous role of Dan Duryea.

Scottish actor Edmond Breon, billed before Duryea, did not have as crucial a role as Duryea but he had a film portfolio dating back to 1907.

Imagine the brouhaha when an agent fights over billing. Pictured right is Breon with his agent who bore a slight resemblance to Joseph Cotten. They are discussing a contract and publicity stills and whether they should shoot someone over Breon's billing.

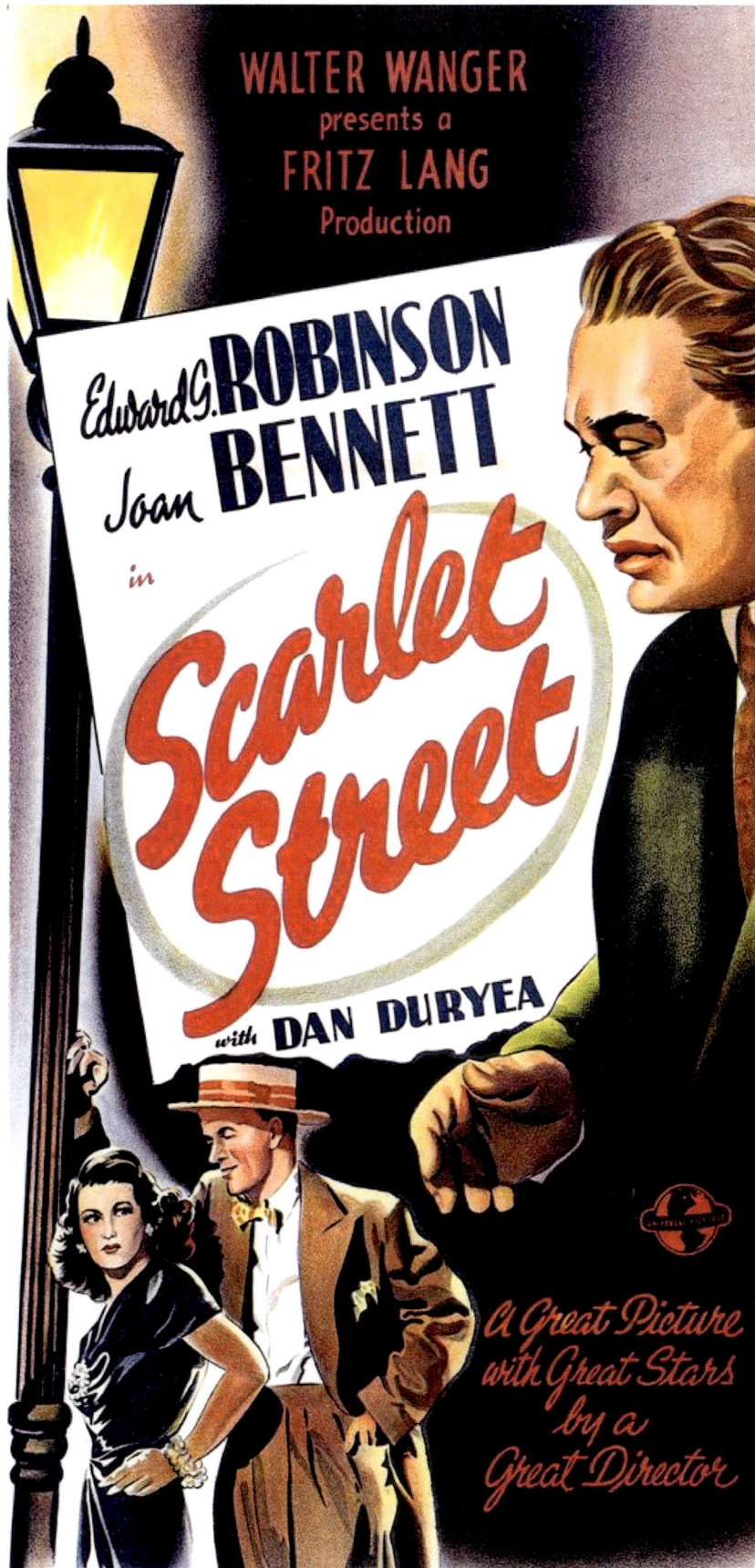

1945

ORSON WELLES'

The Stranger

ORSON WELLES EDWARD G. ROBINSON
LORETTA YOUNG RICHARD LONG

1946

What I cannot have... I'll destroy!

The Red House

1947

1948

1949

With Susan Hayward
Richard Conte
Luther Adler
Director Joseph L. Mankiewicz

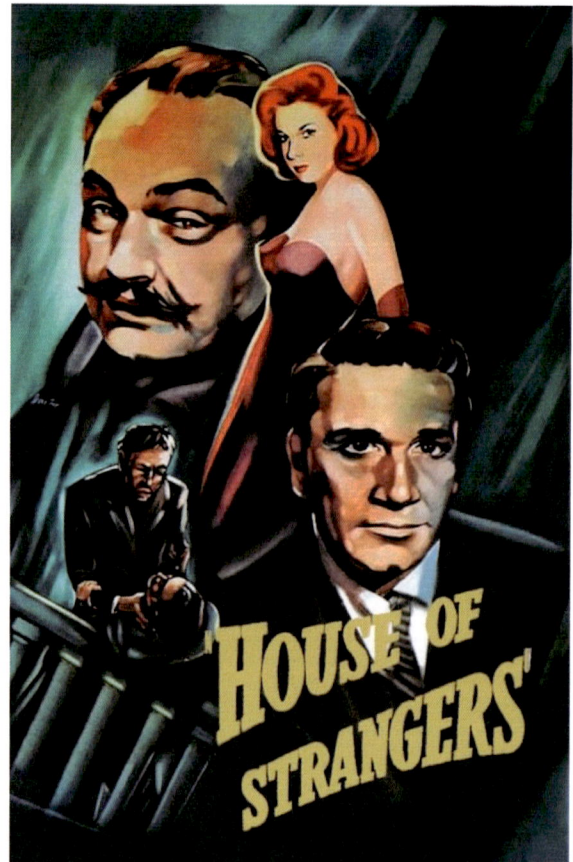

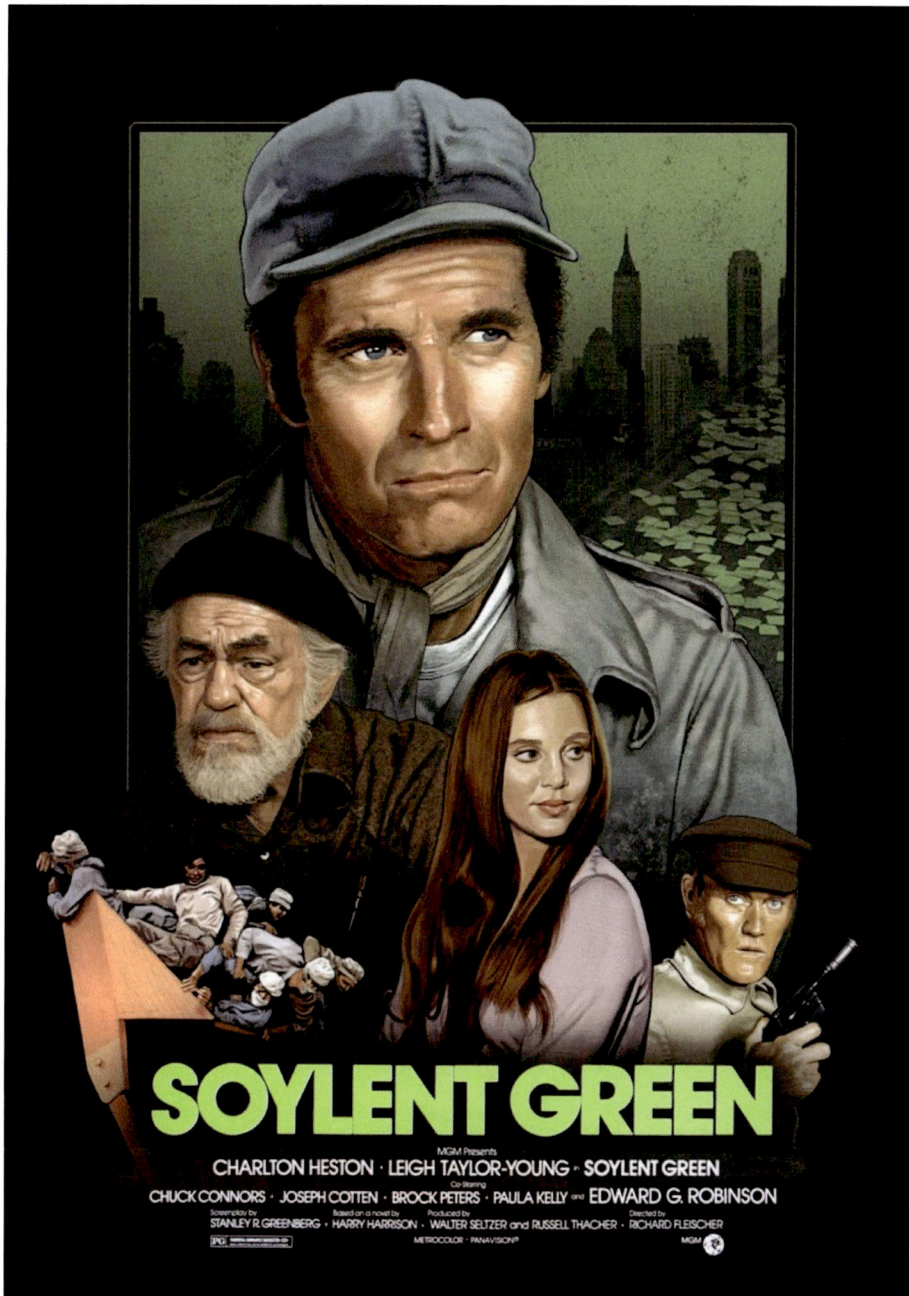

Robinson's films of the 1950s, including noirs and comedies, were adequate, but none was oustanding. The pick of his 50s movies was a noir *Black Tuesday* 1954, with Jean Parker, directed by Argentine Hugo Fregonese.

In the 1960s, Robinson had mostly bit parts. He managed to finish on a high with the sci-fi parable *Soylent Green* 1973.

The Verdict *The Red House*

⭐⭐⭐⭐☆

Crime1938

WHEN I was a young boy, American television comedians would try to make me laugh by saying, in a poor foreign accent, "Come with me to ze Casbah." I could not pick the accent as French, I thought the Casbah was a nightclub, and I had never heard of the 1938 film noir, which was mistakenly attributed as the source of the quote, "Come with me to ze Casbah".

That's right. Just as Humphrey Bogart or Ingrid Bergman never said, "Play it again, Sam" in the 1942 noir adventure *Casablanca*, Frenchman Charles Boyer never invited Hedy Lamarr to come wit' zim to ze Casbah. There is little doubt *Casablanca* owes part of its success to *Algiers* on which it was modelled so it is amusing each film produced a misquote which travelled down the generations.

Algiers, the capital of Algeria, had been a French colonial possession for 100 years when the eponymous 1938 film was made. Morocco became a French "protectorate" in 1912. Algiers is on the Mediterranean Sea and Casablanca is a Moroccan port on the Atlantic Ocean. The main religion of the Native populations of both countries was Islam.

Both being close to Europe (across the sea to Spain) and on major trade routes, they were strategic ports in terms of trade and defence.

Europeans had come to outnumber Muslims in Algiers (though not in Algeria as a whole). Consumers of Hollywood films in America, Europe, Australia, and New Zealand would have known little of these parts of north Africa until they saw *Algiers*, *Casablanca*, or the Bing Crosby-Bob Hope comedy *The Road to Morocco* 1942. World War I veterans who had served in north Africa were the exceptions who had knowledge of the area.

LE CORBUSIER
PLAN OBUS, ALGIERS, 1933

The only other time Algiers was on people's radar in Europe was when French-Swiss architect Le Corbusier proposed in 1931 the building of a second high-rise city above Algiers to make vertical residences more equal than those in rich and deprived areas of horizontal neighbourhoods.

The French Government wanted nothing to do with the idea and by 1938 the Arab Muslim population was still living in the Casbah, the centuries-old hilltop district built below a decaying citadel. The Casbah's intertwining lanes and terraces are basic to the plot of the film *Algiers*.

None of the three films *Algiers*, *Casablanca*, or *The Road to Morocco* was created in the places of their titles. *Casablanca* was a Hollywood film lot, and the Moroccan desert was the Imperial Sand Dunes in Southern California. The closest to geographic authenticity was *Algiers* as producer Walter Wanger sent a London photographer to take still shots of Algiers which were spliced into the moving picture.

Boyer and Lamarr: The sadness in Gaby's eyes portends a doomed romance.

Algiers is a close remake of the 1937 French film *Pépé le Moko*, the title character played by Charles Boyer in the American version. Pépé is a French jewel thief, hiding out for two years in the Casbah where he leads a small gang and has an Algerian girlfriend, Ines (Sigrid Gurie). Though French authorities persistently hunt le Moko, they cannot capture him as he always escapes through the labyrinth which is the Casbah.

Wily local detective Inspector Slimane (Joseph Calleia) knows le Moko can only be captured if he is lured out of the Casbah by his love for beautiful French tourist Gaby (Hedy Lamarr),

That plot outline might not sound like it, but *Algiers* is a gritty noir. The dominant theme is betrayal and fidelity. The secondary theme of the loneliness of the Colons (colonizers) far from home is not convincing nor compelling.

Joe and Sig: Joseph Calleia, right, suspects Sigrid Gurie, centre, is assisting Boyer.

Why the theme of betrayal? Well, producer Walter Wanger was an anti-fascist, director John Cromwell was later blacklisted by the House Un-American Activities Committee 1938-75 (with little evidence) as a communist. Cinematographer James Wong Howe was graylisted for a brief period in the late 1940s as a communist sympathiser.

Fascist political parties, which had support organisations in the United States, controlled Germany, and Italy. Civil war between republicans and fascists/ monarchists raged in Spain, across the sea from Algeria. Betrayal was in the mind of Europeans and U.S. citizens.

During the time between the movies *Algiers* and *Casablanca*, fascist Germany had conquered France and set up a puppet Vichy Government in France and French African colonies.

In *Casablanca* Claude Rains plays a reluctant cynical administrator of the Vichy government.

The 1966 Italian-Algerian film *Battle of Algiers* tells the story of the 1956-57 battle between French colonizers and resistance fighters who took over the Casbah.

Algiers was a hostile environment from the 1930s until the 1960s. Betrayal is also a theme of *Battle of Algiers*.

Scholars suggest *The Maltese Falcon* 1941 was the first film noir. Others cite *Stranger on the Third Floor* 1940 and I will agree with this Peter Lorre film if we determine noir started no earlier than that year.

French film critic Nino Frank coined the term *film noir* in 1946 for war-time American crime films released in France after the war: *The Maltese Falcon* 1941; *Murder, My Sweet* 1944, *Double Indemnity* 1944, and *Laura* 1944. Conservative French critics had described 1930s progressive films that explored class conflict as film noir (bleak film) but they were not describing a genre or kind of film as Nino Frank was.

Critics were right to tie film noir to war but they had the wrong war. Expat European film makers and dramatists (often Jewish) brought to the U.S. the styles of 1920s German Expressionism, a reaction to the horrors of World War I. Noir novelists Dashiell Hammett *The Maltese Falcon* 1930 and Raymond Chandler *The Big Sleep* 1939 incurred chronic injuries in World War I and became alcoholics after it. James M. Cain *The Postman Always Rings Twice* 1934 served in France during WWI. Cain has a credit in *Algiers* for dialogue.

A pre-1940 film such as *Algiers* is sometimes called proto-noir. A literal translation of the Greek prefix proto is first. A protagonist is first on film credits for a movie. I am happy to acclaim the movie *Algiers* as a genuine noir.

Noir: it's a shadowy world.

CHINESE-American cinematographer James Wong Howe was an innovator who achieved the first of his 10 Academy Award nominations for *Algiers*. He won for *The Rose Tattoo* 1955, a dated Italian ethnography but the cinematography still inspires, and the neo-noir Western *Hud* 1963, a hit in its time, but now often forgotten. Howe liked playing with shadows which is one of the hallmarks of noir. The other noir cinematographic genius John Alton called his 1949 manual *Playing with Light*.

Close-ups, another noir trope, are prominent in Algiers. There is one close-up of Lamarr when we wait for long seconds for a change of expression which finally arrives but is difficult to read. The close-up looked more bizarre than evocative, but it stayed in the film.

Cigarettes are smoked constantly to place us in the edgy world of noir.

In the photo above, you will see Howe had already developed the craft of deep focus, in which characters in both foreground and background are in focus. The slouching cynicism of the man leaning on a dresser (Ben Hall) adds to the drama.

The Player

CHARLES BOYER (28 August 1899 – 26 August 1978) was a French actor who spent the 1930s acting in both Hollywood and Paris. He became a U.S. citizen in 1942. Boyer received four Oscar nominations including one for *Algiers* and another for his most famous role in the noir *Gaslight* (1944 with Ingrid Bergman and Joseph Cotten).

Vive la France: In France, Boyer did the crime drama *Tumultes*, directed by later noir doyen Robert Siodmak. Fritz Lang directed him in the fantasy *Liliom* 1934.

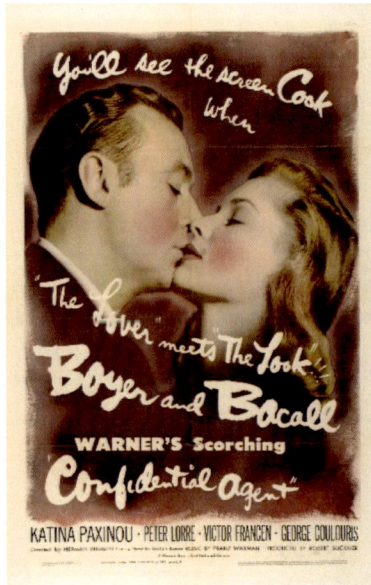

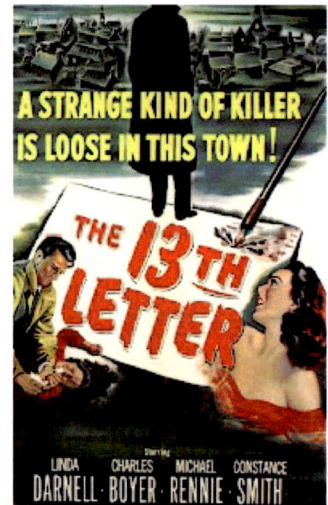

In Hollywood, Boyer played in romances, adventures, and comedies. Besides *Gaslight*, he starred in *Confidential Agent* 1945, beside a disappointing Lauren Bacall, *A Woman's Vengeance* 1948, pursuing a theme popular in Hollywood over the decades, and *The 13th Letter* 1951, directed by Otto Preminger.

Time caught up with Chales Boyer, 78, and Ingrid Bergman, 62, long after their days of monocolor glory. Boyer's last film and Bergman's second-last was *A Matter of Time* 1978. The musical was one of the misses in director Vincente Minnelli's hit-and-miss career. The duo had starred in the wartime romance *Arch of Triumph* 1948.

The Player

Maltese-born Joseph Calleia received the 1938 National Board of Review Award for his performance as Arab Inspector Slimane. It is an attention-grabbing turn with the policeman's wide-open eyes and cane making him seem blind until he says he sees le Moko every day.

The National Board of Review began in New York in 1930 as non-governmental censorship body. It had censorship in its title for years but changed it as it had lofty ambitions to improve cinema which it saw as an admirable democratic art. The National Board of Review Awards began in 1930 and continue to this day.

The National Board of Review Award was a rare cinema accolade for Calleia. Born in 1897, he was a stage star from the mid-1920s, but the film studio system rarely gave him substantial roles.

Even as second lead as a gangster in *Tough Guy* 1936, Calleia was straddled with both nemeses of an actor that comedian W.C. Fields warned against – a child and an animal. It was not just any child, it was Jackie Cooper, the cutest crying-est kid in America. It was not just any animal, it was Rin Tin Tin, the cutest bravest WWI-veteran dog in all of U.S.A.

"Rinty" was only a war vet of sorts as he was rescued as a pup from a battlefield. And he died in 1932. Kind-hearted moguls could not bear to tell the fans, and he was a cash cow, er, dog. Rinty was replaced with stand-ins, bearing his name.

Calleia secured the lead in *Man of the People* 1937, an attempted comedy drama that fell well short of excellence. He was adequate in his subdued interpretation of an honest Italian lawyer whom political fixers try to control. Above, Calleia displays fine facial manipulation to express humiliation when he must bargain with chief fixer Thomas Mitchell. The "Organization" head controls the courts in which Calleia's clients receive unduly harsh verdicts and sentences.

The B-movie's main problem is that the screenplay, including trite dialogue, lets Calleia and the other actors down. ★★★☆☆

Calleia's acting ability deserved better film vehicles throughout his career, but Hollywood outcast Orson Welles redeemed the industry a little when he cast 60-year-old Calleia in the role of naïve cop Pete Menzies in *A Touch of Evil* 1958.

Menzies is a central character in this late film noir as he represents the public and media, deluded by a larger than life public figure with the gift of the gab to reconstruct realty. Sound familiar? The real magic of the Golden Age of Hollywood is its ability to speak to audiences of 70 years later. It is a pity we did not find the golden eggs of wisdom hidden in the flashy entertainment.

The Player

Sigrid Gurie (1911-1969) was born in Brooklyn to Norwegian parents and raised in Oslo.

Gurie returned to the United States in 1936 and, two years later, she landed her first credited role in the juicy part of Pépé's Arabian lover, Ines, in *Algiers*.

With limited training she was plunged into lead roles in *The Adventures of Marco Polo* 1938, and *The Forgotten Woman* 1939. By the time she was panned for her performance opposite John Wayne in *Three Faces West* 1940, Gurie was indeed the forgotten woman after receiving high praise for *Algiers*.

Gurie was the female lead in *Voice in the Wind* 1944 an unusual but good noir directed by Arthur Ripley. Ripley was a comedy writer for Mack Sennett in the 1920s and a director of W.C. Fields comedies in the 1930s. Ripley followed the sombre lyrical antifa *Voice in the Wind* with the quirky noir *The Chase* 1946, spoiled by an unsatisfactory ending.

Voice in the Wind shooter was Richard Fryer who shot popular serials such as *The Perils of Pauline* 1933, *Flash Gordon* 1936, and *Black Arrow* 1944.

I love *Voice in the Wind* which has never been restored. It is crying out for restoration. ★★★★☆

Sigrid Gurie gave up acting for art and jewellery making in the late 1940s.

Good line

Voice in the Wind bartender (Luis Alberni): Pernod (the liqueur) is no good for anyone. It makes you play the piano and I don't like the piano. I hate the piano.

The production of Pernod, distilled from absinthe, a form of wormwood, was banned in France from 1915 but continued in Spain. Artists who admired and avidly consumed Pernod included Van Gogh, Toulouse Lautrec (see the Green Fairy in Baz Luhrmann's *Moulin Rouge* 2001) and Oscar Wilde. The bartender's tale of pernicious Pernod is a delightful intro to *Voice in the Wind*. What follows is one of the longest and certainly most elegiac preludes to a noir flashback.

77

ALAN HALE SNR is Grandpere, a member of le Moko's gang, who spends much of the film smoking hashish through a water pipe. Alan Hale Jnr is best remembered as the Skipper in the television show *Gilligan's Island* 1964–1967. Bob Denver, who played Gilligan, was found guilty of possessing marijuana in 1971 and in 1998 but did no jail time on either conviction. Hale Jnr was in the 1954 noir *Rogue Cop*, starring Robert Taylor, Janet Leigh, and George Raft. Chain smoker Robert Taylor died of lung cancer at the age of 57, proving drugs will indeed kill you.

Poetic realism

POETIC REALISM was a movement in 1930s French film where the lives of people on the margins of society were partially represented in lyrical metaphors. The French original *Pépé le Moko* 1937, directed by Julien Duvivier, used poetic realism and so does the American copy. An example is the scene when Pépé leaves the Casbah for the last time, and his mind is awash with visions of Paris.

With the fall of France to the Germans in 1940, Duvivier and *Pépé le Moko* lead Jean Gabin escaped to Hollywood. Gabin starred in the noir *Moontide* 1942 with Ida Lupino and Claude Rains. *Moontide* used poetic realism.

Duvivier directed five films in America. The only noir was *Destiny* 1944 and he was uncredited as his contribution was retrieved from the cutting-room floor of another of his films.

Financials

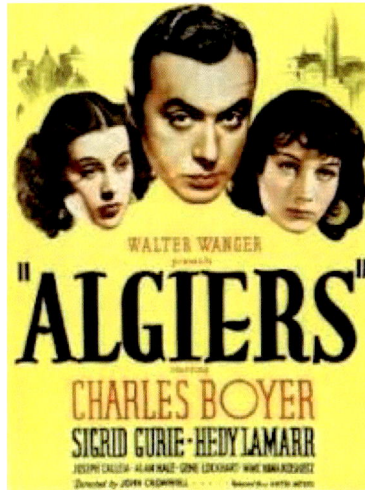

Among my favourite noirs are low-budget B-pictures where imagination and skill made up for lack of budget. *Algiers* was medium budget. It cost $692,000 to make – $15.6m in 2025 money and returned $21.4m in 2025 values. Figures are in USD.

Blockbusters with ridiculous budgets of $200-450 million are an invention of the past 20 years. The accountants are getting more creative and filmmakers less so. Small comedies are easier to make than small dramas.

In 2025 money, *Star Wars* 1977 cost less than $57m and returned a gross of $4.06 billion. Impressive! How about *Gone with the Wind* 1939 which returned a gross of $8.9 billion, in 2025 values, on a budget of $88m in 2025 dollars.

The Verdict *Algiers*

★★★⯪☆

Crime 1953

In All Its Fury and Violence ...Like No Other Picture Since "SCARFACE" and "LITTLE CAESAR"!

"THE KILLING"

starring Sterling HAYDEN

co-starring COLEEN GRAY · VINCE EDWARDS with JAY C. FLIPPEN · MARIE WINDSOR · TED DeCORSIA

Based on the novel "Clean Break," by Lionel White · Screenplay by Stanley Kubrick · Produced by James B. Harris

Directed by Stanley Kubrick · Released thru United Artists

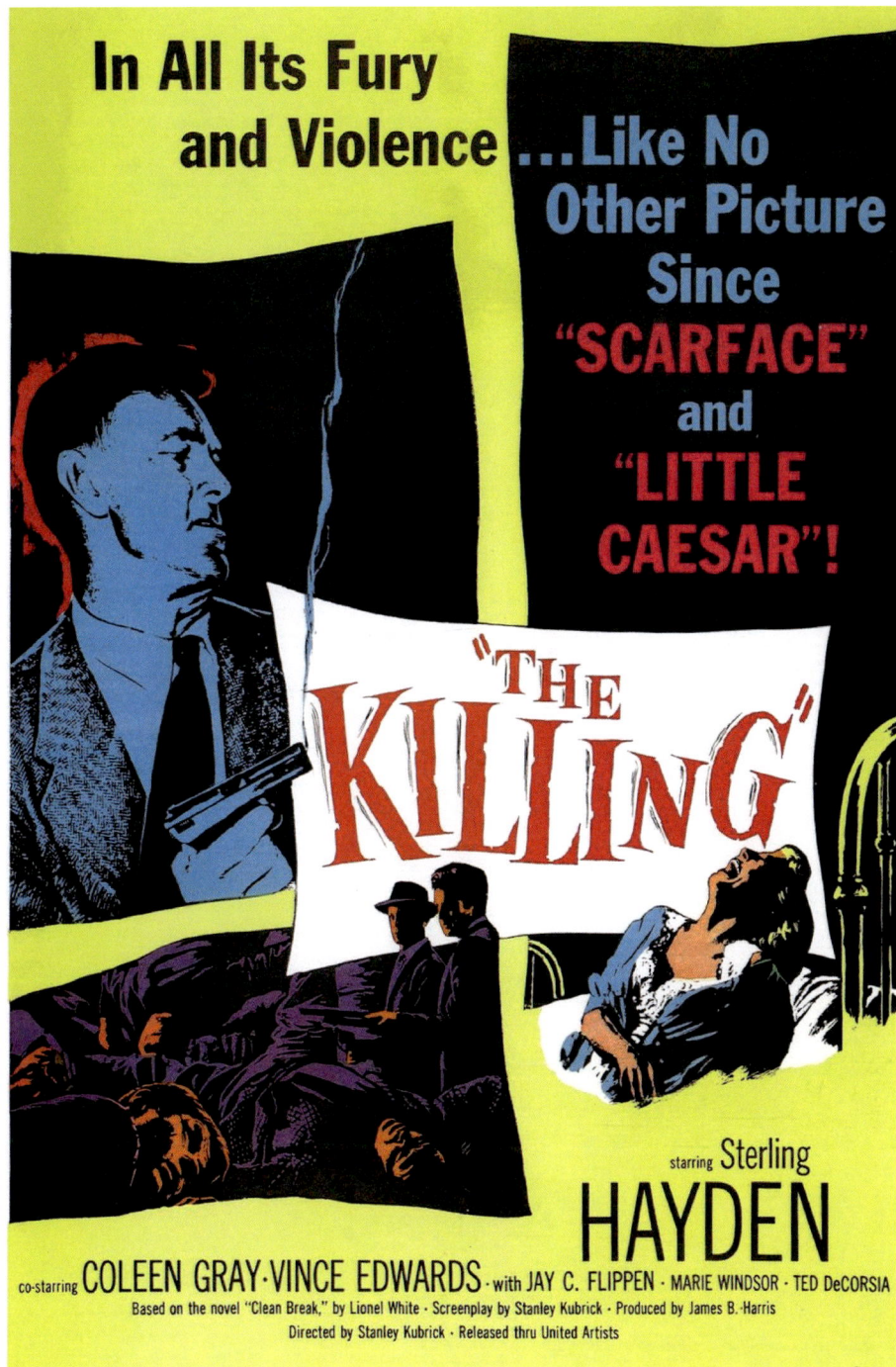

The second and third feature films of auteur Stanley Kubrick were the noirs, *Killer's Kiss* 1953 and *The Killing* 1956. Neither is in the public domain, but Kubrick's initial feature is, and its gross failings led to the ambitious New Yorker's foray into two good noirs that introduced the great filmmaker to the world. Kubrick was not interested in making another noir after *Killer's Kiss* and *The Killing*. Yet most, if not all, of his subsequent films have a theme eminently realizable in a noir: toxic masculinity, born of insecurity, kills.

There are eight million stories in the naked city of New York. This is one of them.

Violent insecurity: In *Killer's Kiss*, Frank Silvera plays a deadly dance-club owner rejected by an employee.

For *Killer's Kiss* Frank Silvera, as Vincent Rapallo, receives top billing, even though he is the antagonist to Jamie Smith's protagonist, Davey Gordon.

Frankly Stacey: Frank Silvera played Stacey Marshall in the first Western directed by Budd Boetticher and the director's first film in color.

A respected stage actor on and off-Broadway since the 1930s, Silvera made his film debut as a bit player in the low-budget Western *The Cimarron Kid* 1952 with Audie Murphy and directed by Budd Boetticher in his first attempt at a genre for which he became renowned (*Seminole* 1953, *The Man from the Alamo* 1953, *Ride Lonesome* 1959, one of seven of the director's movies starring Randolph Scott, and the TV series *Maverick* 1957 and *The Rifleman* 1961).

Frank Silvera was largely unknown to film audiences when he accepted a role in his fifth film which was Stanley Kubrick's first full-length feature.

Silvera was the pick of a bad bunch of actors in the anti-war adventure drama, *Fear and Desire* 1952. Silvera, with 20 years on the stage and four films behind him, was by far the most experienced person on the set of *Fear and Desire*, directed, shot, and edited by 25-year-old Stanley Kubrick. Top billing in Kubrick's second feature was compensation for being part of the director's embarrassment that Kubrick abandoned into the public domain.

The title *Fear and Desire* was strange for a war movie and was not Kubrick's choice. The acting was bad, and the script was worse. The scriptwriter was Kubrick classmate Howard Sackler who went on to write a hit 1967 play *The Great White Hope* which became a hit 1970 movie.

The blending of arthouse and exploitation in *Fear and Desire* was downright weird. The movie failed to work on so many levels.

He could beat any white man
in the world.
He just couldn't beat all of them.

From the play and performances that won the Pulitzer Prize, The New York Critics Award and The Tony Award

20th Century-Fox Presents A Lawrence Turman-Martin Ritt Production.

The Great White Hope

Starring James Earl Jones, Jane Alexander.

Produced by Lawrence Turman. Directed by Martin Ritt.
Screenplay by Howard Sackler based on his play.
Produced on the New York Stage by Herman Levin. PANAVISION® Color by DE LUXE®   GP

Sackler wrote the screenplay for *Killer's Kiss*, but he was uncredited for unknown reasons. Kubrick received credit for the story

DE STANLEY KUBRICK
el beso del ASESINO
(KILLER'S KISS)

Kubrick was rightly embarrassed by his first full-length feature that failed to recoup its modest budget. The director was rumored to have burned the negative and he tried unsuccessfully to round up all the prints to destroy them (Hutchinson, S. *Fear and Desire: The Movie Stanley Kubrick Didn't Want You to See, Mental Floss* online, Apr 6, 2017).

The discipline of film noir quickly set his career back on track. He was still learning the trade with *Killer's Kiss*. As with his first feature he over-extended himself on writing (with an uncredited Howard Sackler and star Frank Silvera) production, direction, cinematography, editing, and post-production. But he constrained his arty flourishes within a traditional film noir structure.

Attractively photographed scenes impress throughout the film which climaxes with an exciting and innovative chase and fight scenes. The elemental noir theme of the hunted in peril in the uncaring big city plays out well in *Killer's Kiss*.

Who's that? Suspense builds when Irene Kane and Jamie Smith hear someone at the door.

Axe-tion: The big fight scene is in a mannequin factory. Was Kubrick commenting on male violence against women or did he want cheap gratuitous nudity? Who knows?

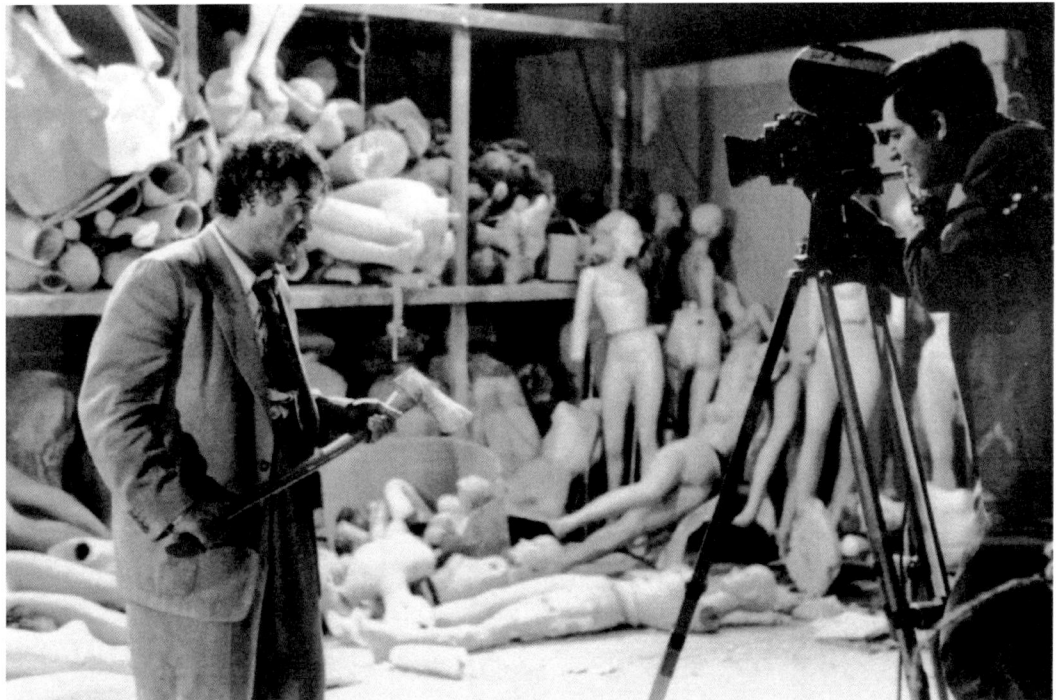

Kubrick's camera work was adept. He knew about the light and shade of chiaroscuro lighting, capturing threatening architecture, and jagged angles. But he was no John Alton or James Wong Howe when it came to shooting noir.

Ever the perfectionist, Kubrick composed scenes a little too neatly. The sign "watch your step" is so obvious you wonder if Kubrick meant it as a sight gag. Kubrick said the sign was there and he liked the serendipity of that.

Even though noir techniques and motifs abound, much of the time, it does not look like we are watching a gritty noir in *Killer's Kiss*.

The most authentically noirish scene and one of the best in the film is the murder in an alley.

Whatever its shortcomings as noir, Kubrick's second feature *Killer's Kiss* is an entertaining suspenseful film.

One sequence should have tipped off an observant viewer to Kubrick's future greatness. Sophisticated critics refer to such a sequence as contingency in Kubrick. I prefer to see it as the whimsy of Fate.

Two street performers appear in the middle of a tense scene. At first, we viewers think they provide light background like comic relief in a Shakespearean tragedy.

Kubrick persists in showing them but never in close-up.

One steals Davey Gordon's scarf and runs away with it. We in the audience are begging Davey not to run after him; it is only a scarf. But he does not listen to us.

All hell is about to break loose. We know it. But Davey does not.

Distributor United Artists offered to buy the film for $100,000. UA would also kick in another $100,000 towards Kubrick's next film. But – there's always a but in Hollywood – the auteur would have to change the ending.

Kubrick agreed to change the ending. It did not ruin the movie, but it did not fit with the stylistics that went before either.

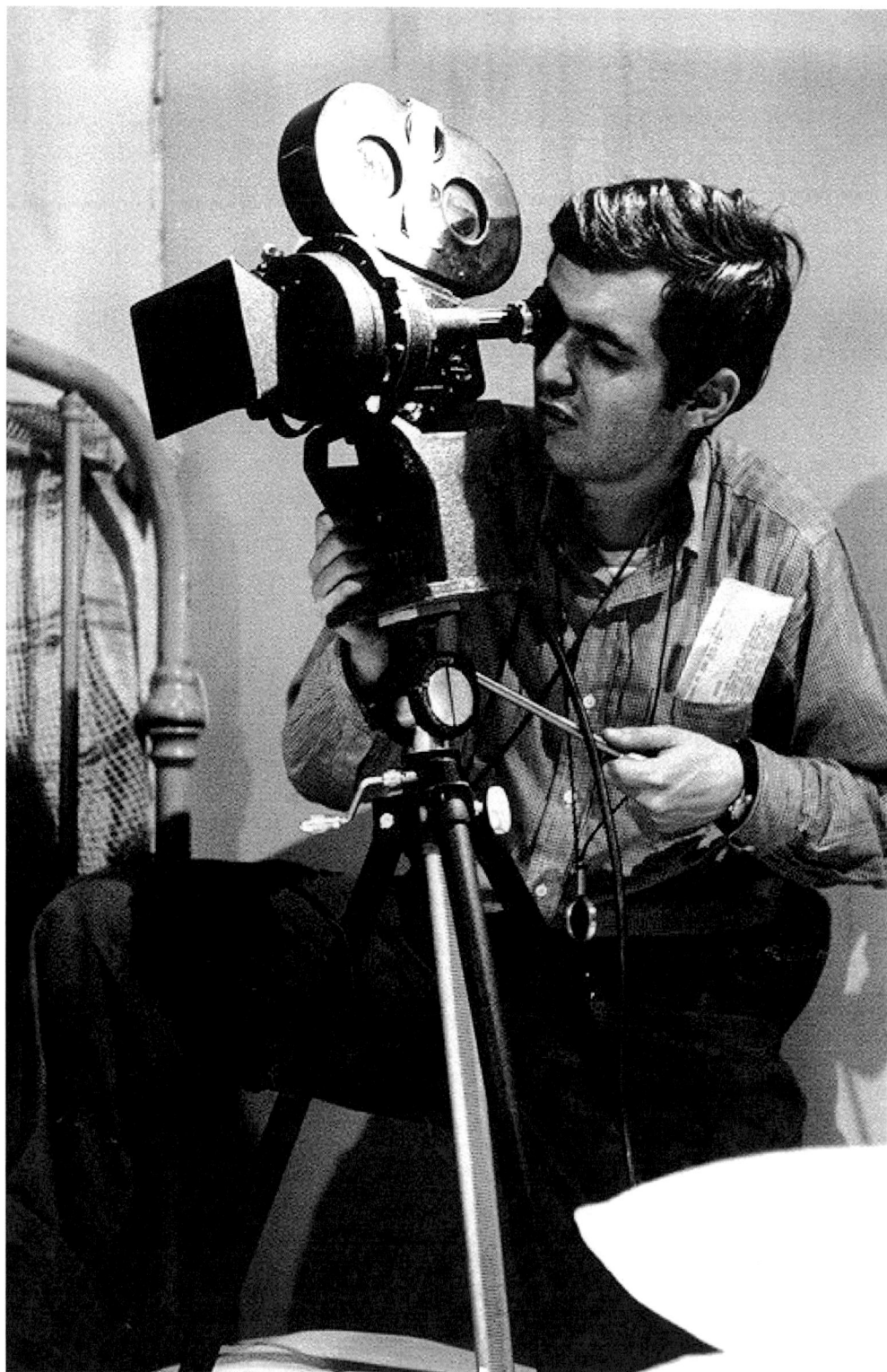

Young **STANLEY KUBRICK** gave up his job as a photographer with *Look* magazine to start the precarious profession of movie production.

At *Look*, Kubrick specialized in photographing boxers and jazz musicians. In *Killer's Kiss*, protagonist Davey is a boxer at the end of his disappointing career. The movie's boxing scene is well done while Kubrick's later films are noted for how well-chosen music enhances the storytelling.

Kubrick's partner at the time of *Killer's Kiss* was professional ballet dancer Ruth Sobotka, a prominent member of the New York avant-garde. Kubrick cast Sobotka as Iris, the dancer sister of female lead character Gloria. In a flashback within the main flashback, Iris dances while Gloria tells a most unpleasant story.

The ballet scene added little to *Killer's Kiss*, but the talented Sobotka had a significant role as art director of Kubrick's next noir *The Killing*.

The couple married between the two films but separated once Kubrick's career looked like taking off. In some ways, the auteur was conservative and expected Sobotka to be content to become a housewife. She left their marital home in Los Angeles to return to New York and her ballet career.

Active in dual careers of acting and costume design, Sobotka died mysteriously in 1967, aged 42. The cause of her death remains unknown.

The verdict *Killer's Kiss*

★★★★☆

Cringe 1956

The humiliation of a rejected dance-club owner was the spur to violence in *Killer's Kiss* and Kubrick continues the cringe theme in his third feature *The Killing*. What better lead than Sterling Hayden, he of the hangdog demeanor that belied his big build. And what better support than the Antihero of Humiliation, Elisha Cook Jr. That Cook did not gain a position on the film poster is a travesty and a repeat of earlier omissions in promotions for *The Maltese Falcon* 1941 and *The Big Sleep* 1946.

To "make a killing" is gambling and corporate slang for making a quick huge profit on a bet or deal. It dates to the 1800s in the United States and could have derived from reporting a big hunting haul or vanquishing an opponent. Either way, it is an unpleasant metaphor.

Gunsight: Fate has Johnny Clay (Sterling Hayden) in its sights though femme fatale Sherry Peatty (Marie Windsor) does not see the danger.

United Artists had promised $100,000 towards Kubrick's third film but before stumping up the cash, they wanted a marquee name to star.

STARRING

STERLING HAYDEN · LOUIS CALHERN

JEAN HAGEN · JAMES WHITMORE · SAM JAFFE

JOHN McINTIRE · a JOHN HUSTON production

Screen Play by BEN MADDOW and JOHN HUSTON · From a Novel by W. R. BURNETT · A METRO-GOLDWYN-MAYER PICTURE

Directed by JOHN HUSTON · Produced by ARTHUR HORNBLOW JR.

Sterling Hayden was not a box-office cash cow but the tall languid, yet crisp-talking actor, was superb in the classic heist noir *The Asphalt Jungle* (1950, directed by John Huston with a breakout role for Marilyn Monroe). Kubrick suggested Hayden and United Artists agreed with reservations.

THE KILLING, director Stanley Kubrick, Vince Edwards, Marie Windsor

Novice and two pros: Newbie Kubrick with Vince Edwards (*Rogue Cop* 1954, *Cell 2455 Death Row* 1955, and *The Night Holds Terror* 1955) and Marie Windsor (*Force of Evil* 1948, *The Sniper* 1952, *The Narrow Margin* 1952, and *City that Never Sleeps* 1953).

In the above photo, Kubrick, pictured left, discusses the movie with Vince Edwards and Marie Windsor. Kubrick had a lifelong habit of consulting with all his actors, but he was much less collegiate with crews. His falling out with actors usually stemmed from his perfectionist insistence of multiple takes than could run into the dozens.

Sherry is married to George, played by everyone's favorite noir patsy, Elisha Cook Jr. who is credited without the Jr. in this and later films. His is the biggest role I have seen Cook play. Personal failings and the whimsy of Fate combine to destroy George. With his weak character, poor choices, and being supernatural Fate's plaything, Cook has the more traditional role of the protagonist in a tragedy than Hayden who gets kicked in the teeth by Fate repeatedly, just because. George is ripe for humiliation.

From his earliest scenes, we viewers have a pitiful sympathy for George as he tries to win back his wife's love that we suspect was never there in the first place. We know it is going to end badly for George and can only shake our heads when he reveals the heist plan to his wife.

Kubrick cleverly mimics the style of a police-procedural film in voice-over and repetitious bass-driven music. The baddies, including a rogue cop, replace police officers. The voice-over uses their first names. This enhances identification with the crooks, but the astute viewer knows they will lose in the end to satisfy the censors.

The action scenes are exciting as with the one started by Vince Edwards (later television's Dr. Ben *Casey* 1961-66, alongside Sam Jaffe who had a memorable role in Hayden's previous heist film, *The Asphalt Jungle*. The scene where voyeur Jaffe risks arrest to look at teenagers dancing is one of my noir favorites).

Before he transformed into Dr. Casey, Edwards scoffed at, "first, do no harm" in *The Killing*.

One Kubrick innovation was to have multiple long intercuts to show what was happening at various places at the same time during the heist. It works a treat, but it may have confused or annoyed viewers used to linear narratives.

The crucial "whimsy of Fate" scene involves a small dog and is excellent.

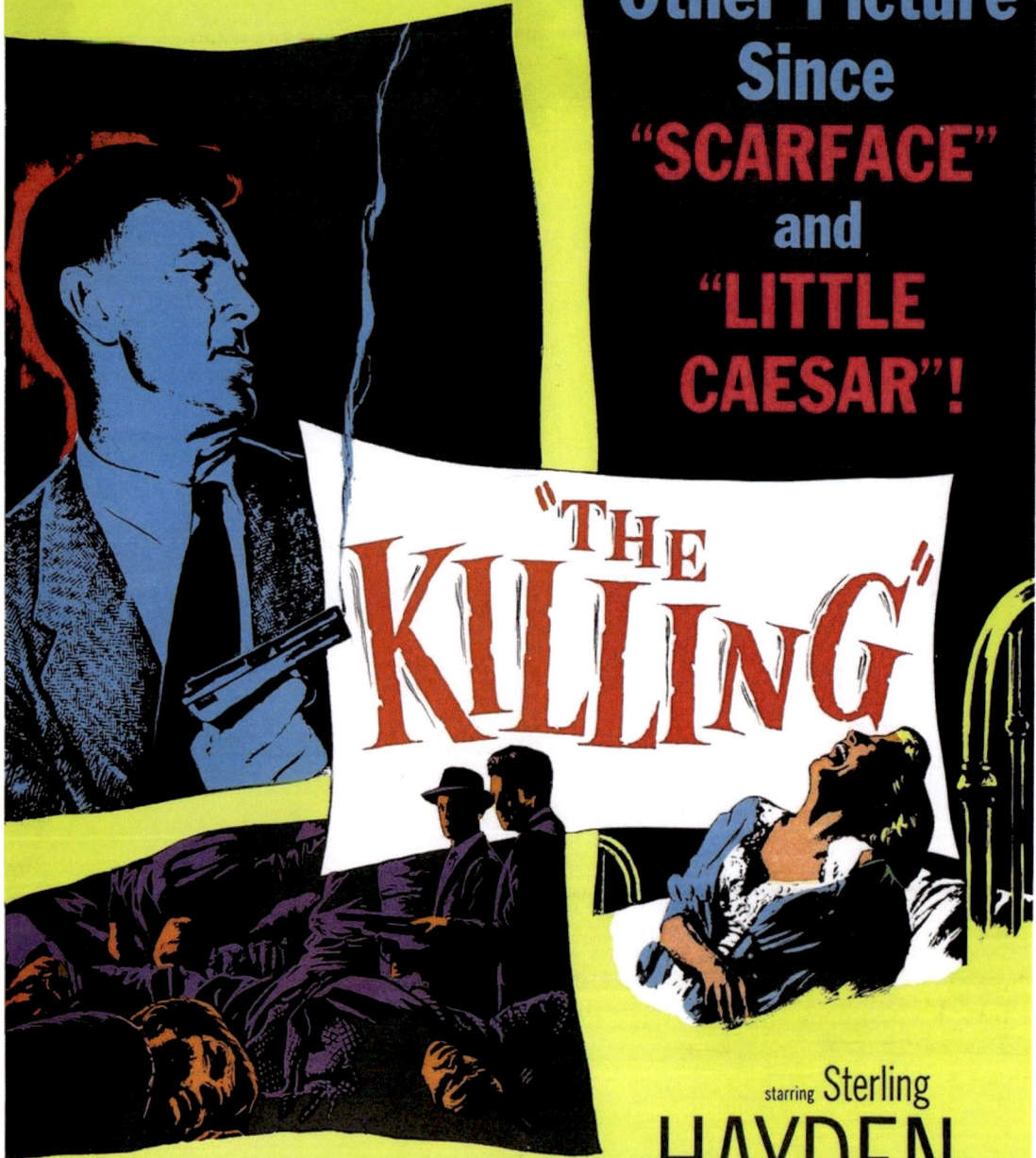

Mistake: Given Kubrick's innovations, marketing *The Killing* by linking it to films of two decades prior would seem a misstep by distributor United Artists.

The Killing, poorly distributed in general, lost money. But Kubrick's talents were on display for all movie makers to see.

Kubrick's increase in expertise from his first dud film to his second good film to his third exceptionally good film was remarkable.

Sterling Hayden respected the way the director shot the movie. "I loved the way the camera was always moving, and we were moving, everything was moving." (1970s interview for French television, uploaded 1 April 2023 by the Stanley Kubrick Appreciation Society).

With complimentary reviews and Hollywood producers taking notice, *The Killing* ended well for Kubrick belying the film's final words uttered exquisitely by Sterling Hayden: "What's the difference?"

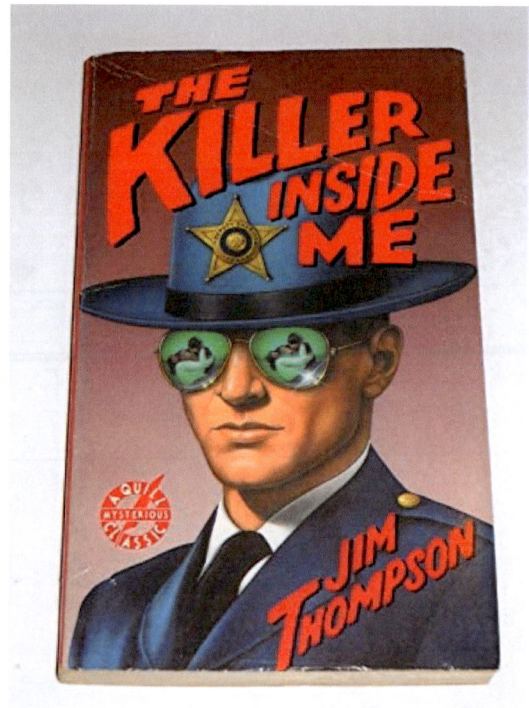

Not only did Kubrick employ experienced noir second-stringers as supports, he hired pulp fiction writer Jim Thompson to pen the screenplay. Thompson's hard-boiled novel *The Killer Inside Me* impressed Kubrick.

The pair worked well together but Thompson was distressed when he saw an early print of the film gave him credit only as the dialogue writer.

Thompson did not raise the issue with Kubrick to ask for an amended credit. As it turned out, Thompson's name was not on the movie poster which had Kubrick as the director and screenplay writer. It was a blow for Thompson whom the demon drink was elating and punishing.

"PATHS OF GLORY"

RALPH MEEKER · ADOLPHE MENJOU with GEORGE MACREADY · WAYNE MORRIS · RICHARD ANDERSON · Screenplay by STANLEY KUBRICK, CALDER WILLINGHAM and JIM THOMPSON · Based on the Novel by HUMPHREY COBB · Directed by STANLEY KUBRICK · Produced by JAMES B. HARRIS · A Bryna Production · Released thru UA UNITED ARTISTS

Jim Thompson received compensation when Kubrick asked him to write his next feature for a good salary. Only a handful of Thompson's scenes were used in *Paths of Glory*, but the noir author received credit for the screenplay and his name appeared on the poster.

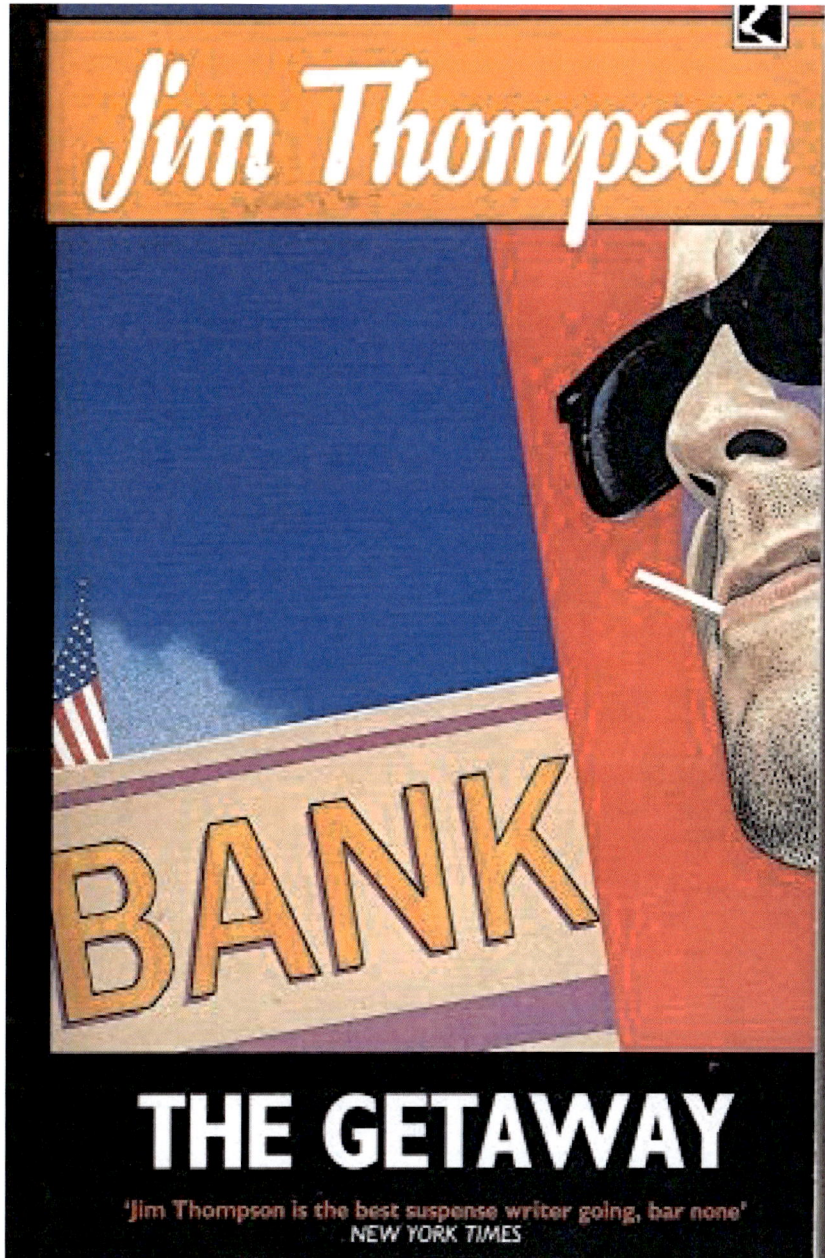

Thompson did not work in Hollywood again until the 1970s. He was hired to write the script for an adaptation of one of his novels. That ended badly.

STEVE **McQUEEN**
ALI **MacGRAW** IN
THE GETAWAY x
A FILM BY SAM PECKINPAH

STEVE McQUEEN
ALI MacGRAW
THE GETAWAY
Co-starring BEN JOHNSON AL LETTIERI and SALLY STRUTHERS as 'Fran'

Jim Thompson worked on the screenplay for *The Getaway* 1972 for four months before his script was rejected for being too wordy and too pessimistic. He was uncredited as a screenwriter, but Thompson claimed the production used much of his material.

Thompson had a small but important part in *Farewell My Lovely* (1975, from Raymond Chandler's novel, with Robert Mitchum as Philip Marlowe). Thompson was the wealthy elderly husband of femme fatale Charlotte Rampling. Thompson died two years later.

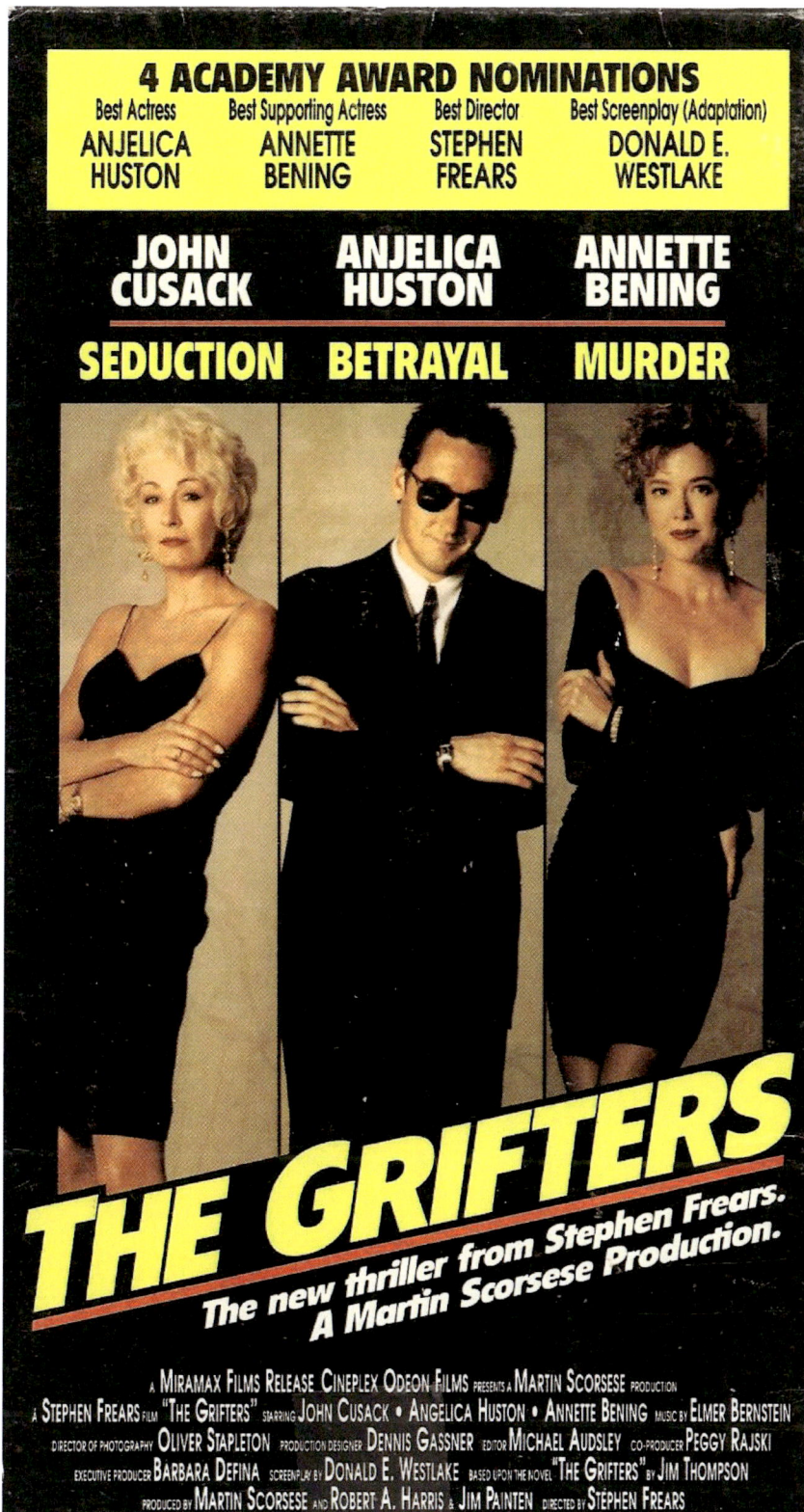

4 ACADEMY AWARD NOMINATIONS

| Best Actress | Best Supporting Actress | Best Director | Best Screenplay (Adaptation) |
| ANJELICA HUSTON | ANNETTE BENING | STEPHEN FREARS | DONALD E. WESTLAKE |

JOHN CUSACK — ANJELICA HUSTON — ANNETTE BENING

SEDUCTION — BETRAYAL — MURDER

THE GRIFTERS

The new thriller from Stephen Frears.
A Martin Scorsese Production.

A MIRAMAX FILMS RELEASE CINEPLEX ODEON FILMS PRESENTS A MARTIN SCORSESE PRODUCTION A STEPHEN FREARS FILM "THE GRIFTERS" STARRING JOHN CUSACK • ANGELICA HUSTON • ANNETTE BENING MUSIC BY ELMER BERNSTEIN DIRECTOR OF PHOTOGRAPHY OLIVER STAPLETON PRODUCTION DESIGNER DENNIS GASSNER EDITOR MICHAEL AUDSLEY CO-PRODUCER PEGGY RAJSKI EXECUTIVE PRODUCER BARBARA DEFINA SCREENPLAY BY DONALD E. WESTLAKE BASED UPON THE NOVEL "THE GRIFTERS" BY JIM THOMPSON PRODUCED BY MARTIN SCORSESE AND ROBERT A. HARRIS & JIM PAINTEN DIRECTED BY STEPHEN FREARS

Another Jim Thompson novel was filmed for release in 1990 with Stephen Frears directing and Martin Scorsese producing. Critics regard *The Grifters* as a neo-noir classic.

Fittingly John Huston's daughter, Angelica, had a lead role. Hint, she's no angel in this one.

MARIE WINDSOR

Marie Windsor played the femme fatale in *Force of Evil* (1948: above, she is with the male lead, John Garfield).

Windsor played the femme fatale in *Two-Dollar Bettor* (1951, a horse-racing noir warning about gambling addiction).

She was the femme fatale in *The Sniper* (1952, an edgy noir, about misogyny, directed by Edward Dmytryk, his first film after returning from being blacklisted). Windsor is pictured with Arthur Franz.

Windsor was the femme fatale in the acclaimed noir *The Narrow Margin* 1952, directed by Richard Fleischer.

Martin M. Goldsmith (novels *Double Jeopardy* 1938 and *Detour* 1939) wrote the screenplay for *The Narrow Margin*. The shades of edginess and ordinariness throughout the plot elevate this B-noir well above budget expectations and inspire A-grade acting from its B-list cast. Windsor gives the best performance of her career. Goldsmith received an Academy Award nomination.

Marie Windsor was a femme fatale in *City That Never Sleeps* (1952, cinematography by John L. Russell who went on to shoot Hitchcock's *Psycho* 1960). Russell photographed Orson Welles' film adaptation of Shakespeare's *Macbeth* 1948, and the noir *Moonrise* 1948.

Marie Windsor was the lead as, of course, a femme fatale, in *No Man's Woman* (1955, directed by Franklin Adreon who directed episodes of classic television Westerns *Cheyenne* 1955-62, *Gunsmoke* 1955-75, *Sugarfoot* 1957-61, *Maverick* 1957-62, *Bat Masterson* 1958-61, and *Tombstone Territory* 1957-60, "Whistle me a tune that will carry me to Tombstone Territory". The town newspaper is the *Tombstone Epitaph*. Tourists were dying to visit).

Critics have suggested the Windsor character, Sherry Peatty, in *The Killing* is a Kubrick misogynist fantasy. Peatty is a greedy conniving disloyal woman whose scheming leads to the downfall of three men. It seems like a sexist caricature, but an unredeemed evil minor character, male or female, is an effective trope in noir. In Kubrick's work, beginning with *Killer's Kiss*, toxic male misogyny has been a theme.

On brand: In *The Killing* Windsor plays the noir trope of the sociopathic supporting character, portrayed in bug-eyed glory by Neville Brand in *D.O.A.* 1950.

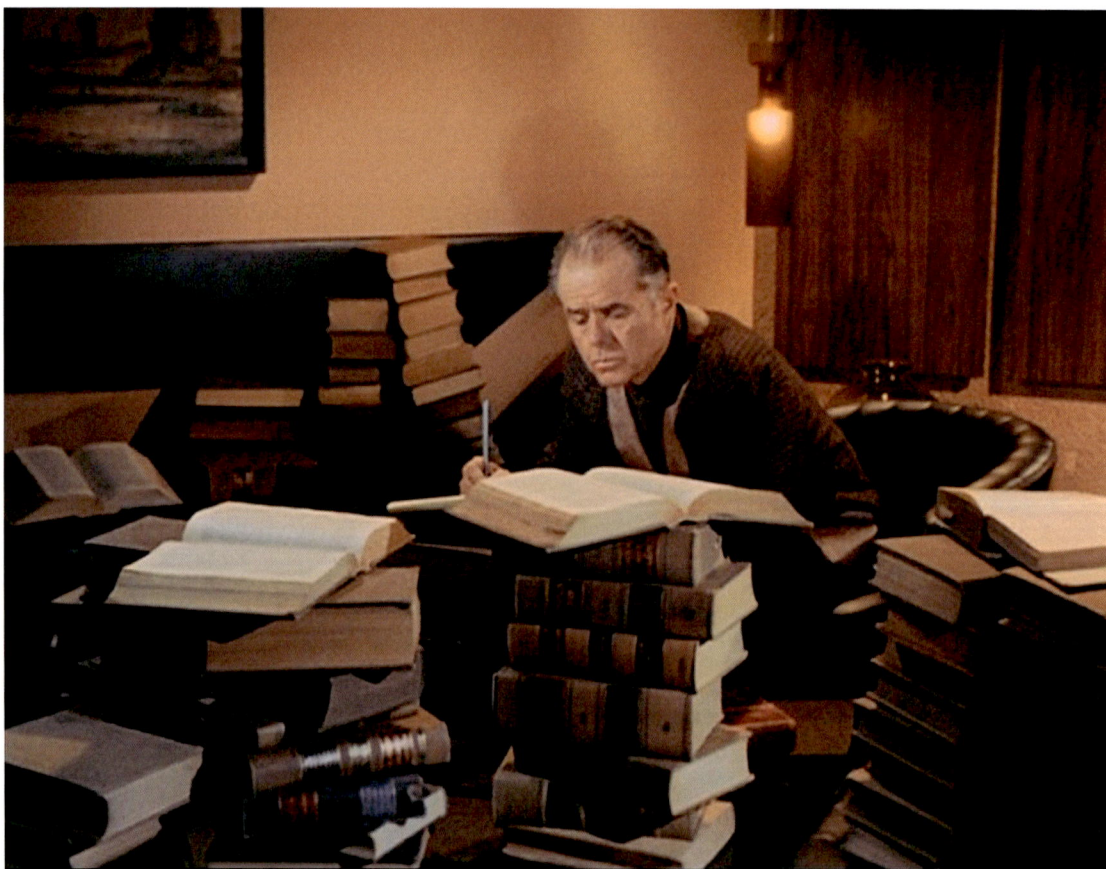

Studious: Intergalactic lawyer Samuel T. Cogley (Elisha Cook Jr.) litigates against an infallible computer in *Court Martial*, 1967, a first season episode of television's *Star Trek: The Original Series* 1966-69.

Scene-stealing (in the nicest way) character actor **ELISHA COOK JR.** burst onto the noir screen from the get-go of film noir in *Stranger on the Third Floor* 1940 followed by *The Maltese Falcon* 1941.

In *The Maltese Falcon* 1941, Cook has a scene-stealing cameo as Wilmer Cook, a psychopathic rent-boy or gunsel as they were called when they were indentured to a criminal such as Kasper Gutman (Sydney Greenstreet). Cook's portrayal shows his viciousness compensates for his psychological weakness compared with the strength of the righteous Sam Spade (Bogart) and the amoral Gutman. Spade repeatedly humiliates Wilmer Cook. Disloyal Gutman agrees to hand him to the Law.

The frightened little boy inside the pretend tough-guy became Cook's stock character in noir and it fascinated viewers. In *The Big Sleep* (1946, again starring Bogart) everything fell into place, right down to the name Harry Jones, for Cook. Jones's scene with Lash Canino (played by Bob Steele) is one of the most memorable in all of noir.

Question time: Is that a huge rat, below right, either out the window or on a painting?

I played the gumshoe and investigated. The jury is still out, but some suggested it reflects a woman on the dance floor.

In between these noirs, Cook gave another iconic performance, though to a different beat, in *Phantom Lady* (1944, directed by Robert Siodmak). He plays intoxicated jazz drummer Cliff, still a loser, simulating a sex act with his kit. Cook's drumming was dubbed.

Fittingly, Cook's noir *Stranger on the Third Floor* (1940, with Peter Lorre) is regarded as Hollywood's first film noir.

Cook's noir immediately after *The Maltese Falcon* was *I Wake Up Screaming* (1941 with Victor Mature and Betty Grable in a departure from her usual comedies and musicals).

Dark Mountain 1944 was a rare miss for Cook as it was a dull rural noir.

Lead Robert Lowery played in more than 70 films, most long forgotten. He did play real-life crime boss Arnold "the Brain" Rothstein in the entertaining gangster movie *The Rise and Fall of Legs Diamond* 1960.

Lowery was third lead in the popular television sentimental adventure series *Circus Boy* 1956-57. Playing the titular role was future member of the Monkees, Micky Dolenz. I follow Micky's positive tweets on X and see he tours still. In true noir fashion, knock 'em dead, Mr Dolenz.

Dark Mountain female lead Ellen Drew had substantial roles in the respected noirs *Johnny O'Clock* 1947 and *The Crooked Way* 1949.

Drew starred in the 1940 screwball comedy *Christmas in July*.

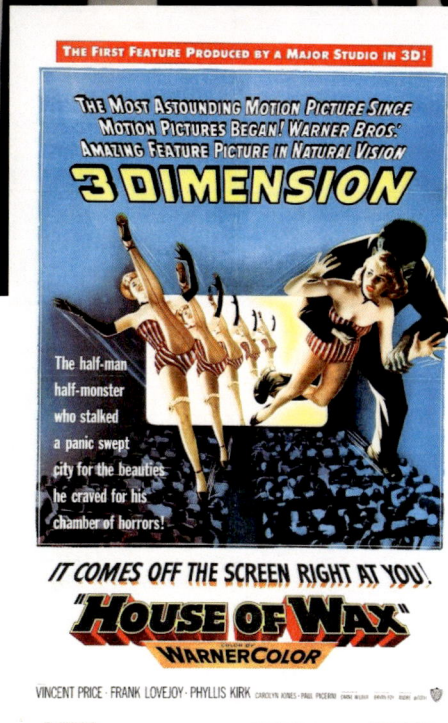

Cook did better with a good role in *Dark Waters* (1944 with Merle Oberon and directed by Andre De Toth, *House of Wax* 1953).

The gangster noir *Dillinger* 1945 was a B-movie smash for Monogram, making at least ten times its budget. A more precise profit figure cannot be made as both budget and box office returns vary from different accounts. Cook is pictured with Mark Lawrence (*Key Largo*, 1948).

Dillinger "introduced" on-screen and off-screen wild-man Lawrence Tierney in the title role. It was Tierney's second credited role after the teen-exploitation movie *Youth Runs Wild* 1944.

UNIVERSAL PRESENTS

BLONDE ALIBI

with Martha O'DRISCOLL
TOM NEAL
DONALD MacBRIDE
ELISHA COOK, JR.
ROBERT ARMSTRONG

The 62-min cheapie *Blonde Alibi* 1946 was a dud.

A dull poster can tip off a moviegoer to the value of an advertised product and the one above lacks signs of the edginess of noir.

Lead O'Driscoll retired the year after *Blonde Alibi*. Her family started The Appleton Museum of Modern Art in Central Florida in 1987. I presume it was an act of atonement for *Blonde Alibi*. Cook atoned in better films.

Another cheapie *Fall Guy* 1947 is of more interest to noiristas as it is better than Cook's previous film and stars Leo Penn, father of actors Sean and the late Chris, and musician Michael. Penn was billed as Clifford in *Fall Guy*.

Leo Penn was blacklisted. His last film before the blacklisting was *Not Wanted* (1949, directed by an uncredited noir favorite Ida Lupino).

Cook was reunited with *Dillinger* lead Lawrence Tierney for the controversial *Born to Kill* 1947, directed by Robert Wise. The co-dependent psychopaths do engage in despicable acts, but this is a well-written, well-acted, and well-made suspenseful noir. Even if you recoil from the unpleasantries, it is hard not to admire the cleverness of this RKO noir.

Despite Cook's significant role, he again was excluded from the poster. He would have been used to the slight by this time.

ROBERT *and* RAYMOND HAKIM *present*

HENRY FONDA
BARBARA BEL GEDDES
VINCENT PRICE
ANN DVORAK

THE LONG NIGHT

An **ANATOLE LITVAK** *production*

Produced by ROBERT and RAYMOND HAKIM
and ANATOLE LITVAK
Directed by ANATOLE LITVAK
Screen Play by JOHN WEXLEY
Based on a story by JACQUES VIOT
RELEASED BY
R K O
RADIO

Despite a stellar cast *The Long Night* 1947 disappointed at the box office.

It was an inferior remake of the French poetic-realist film *Le jour se lève* 1939.

It was karmic for RKO to lose so much money after they had tried to round up and destroy all copies of the French film.

The year 1947 was a good one for the release of Cook noirs. *The Gangster* starred Barry Sullivan and British Olympic figure skater Belita.

I give the filmmakers of *The Gangster* the benefit of a very grave doubt about the sign above and between Belita and Barry Sullivan. Belita Jepson-Turner's other noirs were *Suspicion* 1945, *The Hunted* 1948, and *The Man on the Eiffel Tower* 1949.

If Belita teamed up with Valli, they could have a whole name.

The Hunted was a B-noir of above-average quality typical of the product Allied Artists' parent company Monogram could create. Belita's skating interlude was an authentic alternative to the (usually dubbed) nightclub singing that had infiltrated crime noir.

Before *The Hunted*, Jack Bernhard directed *Violence* 1947, a film about money-grubbing fascists trying to recruit anxious war veterans.

ALLIED ARTISTS PRODUCTION, INC. presents

THE HUNTED

A SCOTT R. DUNLAP PRODUCTION

starring
PRESTON FOSTER and BELITA

PIERRE WATKIN • LARRY BLAKE • RUSSELL HICKS

with PIERRE WATKIN • LARRY BLAKE • RUSSELL HICKS

Associate Producer Glenn Cook • Directed by Jack Bernhard • Story and Screenplay by Steve Fisher

Cook appeared with Zacchary Scott and Dorothy Malone in the oddly titled *Flaxy Martin* 1949.

Dorothy Malone played the flirtatious bookshop manager in that exquisite scene of comic relief in *The Big Sleep* 1946. I paid homage to that scene by creating a similar one in my neo-noir novel, *Iraqi Icicle*. That is not my trying to sneak in product placement. I suppose it is, really, I apologize.

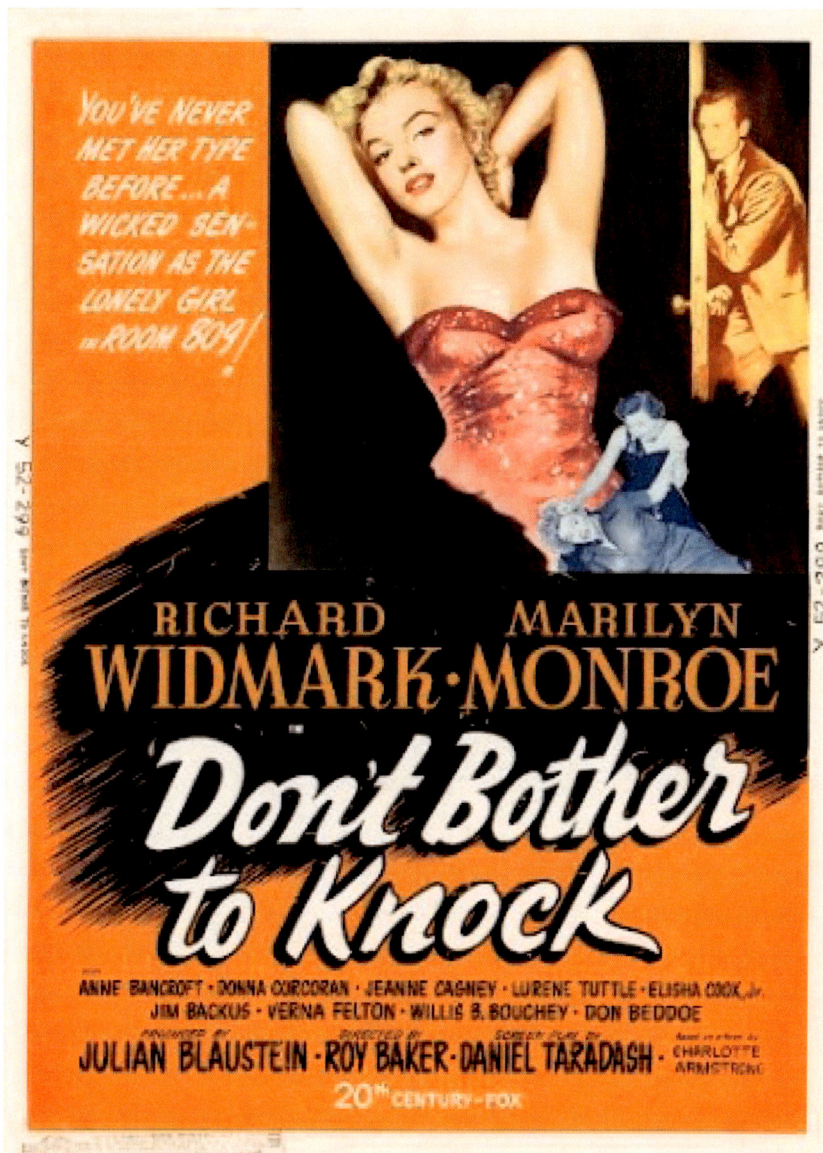

Don't be fooled by Cook's lowly position on the poster. Cook and Marilyn Monroe stole *Don't Bother to Knock* 1952 in their roles as uncle and niece.

Cook followed *The Killing* with the forgettable *Accused of Murder* 1956. This is of most interest to lovers of noir for usually villainous Lee Van Cleef being on the wrong side of the Law, for him, as a police officer.

Chicago Confidential 1957 was no *Kansas City Confidential* 1952 but Cook did get to overplay a character called Candymouth Duggan.

Another heist film beckoned with *Plunder Road* 1957, an innovative B-noir that got big bangs from small bucks.

The gangster noir *Baby Face Nelson* 1957, starring formerly baby-faced Mickey Rooney, followed.

Cook, 53, played Homer Van Meter who, in real life, was 28 when police killed him.

Cook may have died but at least he made the poster. In small print. For some reason, Jr. returned as an addendum to his credit.

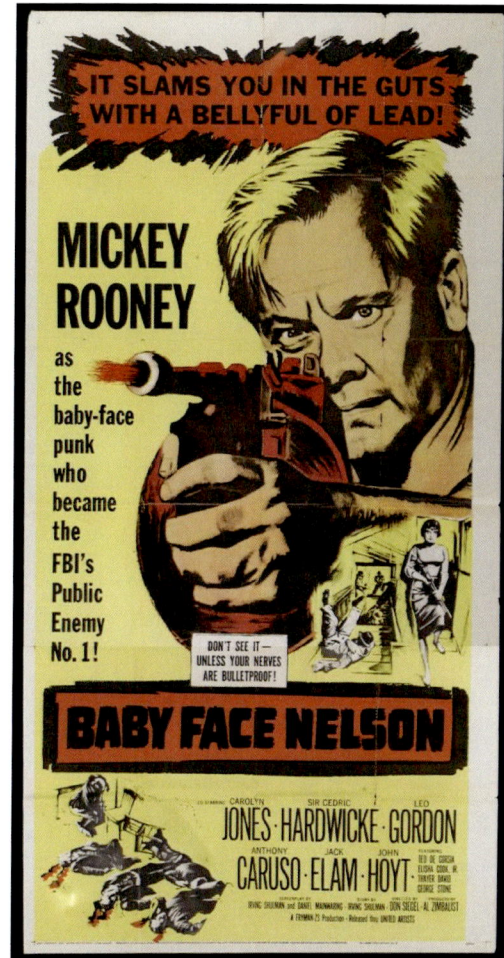

Classical noir was on its last reel by 1958 and Cook's next movie in the genre was the neo-noir, *Johnny Cool* 1963, with Elizabeth Montgomery , as the femme fatale. It was a shallow movie to remind you how good it was not to be one of the cool kids. On reflection Cook and Joseph Calleia would have been glad they had only bit parts in this pretentious travesty.

Elizabeth Montgomery was the daughter of Robert Montgomery who starred in the noirs, *The Lady in the Lake*, and *The Pink Horse*, both 1947. Elizabeth was an outspoken liberal while Robert was a staunch Republican.

Robert Montgomery directed and starred in *The Lady in the Lake* based on a Raymond Chandler novel. The director used the "revolutionary" technique of the camera being gumshoe Philip Marlowe who is rarely seen except as a mirror image as in the above scene with Audrey Totter. Hollywood put the hype into hyperbole and *The Lady in the Lake* was not the first film to use subjective point of view or I-camera. French director Abel Gance used it in *Napoléon* 1927.

Montgomery was the first to use it for a whole film. It sort of works, and the film turned a modest profit despite negativity from critics. But it was a gimmick that was not needed as first-person voice-overs served the same purpose. Or as critic Walter Kerr wrote in his three-word review of the Broadway play *I am a Camera* 1951, "Me no Leica."

Montgomery's more impressive noir was *Ride the Pink Horse* 1947. It is the story of a terse bitter war veteran who rides a Greyhound into the Hispanic city of San Pablo California during the Fiestas de Santa Fe in September. He is on a mission of revenge against an America that cannot provide him with safety and security after his war service. How this movie consistently evades lists of best noirs is an enduring mystery.

No concealed drugs: Admit you thought the film title was a drug reference when you first saw it. I did. It is, in fact, a spiritual allusion. Aren't you ashamed of yourself? I am.

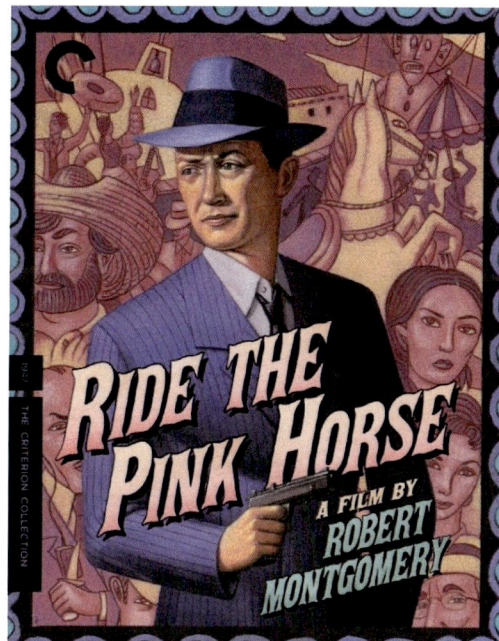

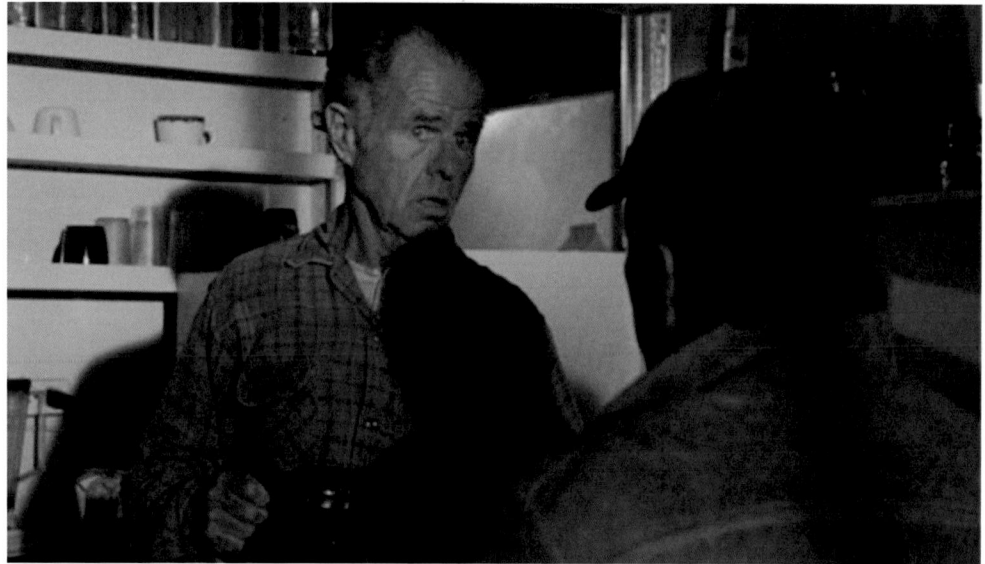

A decade passed after *Johnny Cool* before Cook's next neo-noir *The Outfit* 1973. What memories would have been exchanged at the food van on the set of that movie. Among the supporting cast were Marie Windsor and Timothy Carey from *The Killing*. Robert Ryan (*Crossfire* 1949; *Act of Violence* 1949) had a larger part in *The Outfit*. Ryan made four films released in that year of 1973, the year of his death.

Jane Greer, the iconic femme fatale from the classic *Out of the Past* (1947, pictured with Robert Mitchum) was in the supporting cast of *The Outfit*. Greer was good but she could not throw a stick for a dog to save her life. If Kubrick were directing, he would have made her do it fifty times.

Cook reprised his role of Wilmer Cook for *The Black Bird* (1975, a mirthless spoof of *The Maltese Falcon*). Cook is pictured with George Seagal who plays Sam Spade Jr.

Cook still had "the look" in the tear-jerker *The Champ* (1979, directed by Franco Zeffirelli and sometimes classified as neo-noir). Cook seems to be asking, "How did this dud weepie make so much money?"

Unfortunately, Cook's final neo-noir *Hammett* 1982 was a box-office flop despite direction by celebrated German Wim Wenders and production by Francis Ford Coppola. Frederic Forrest and Marilu Henner are pictured with Cook.

I liked this quirky tale which turns noir author Dashiell Hammett (*Red Harvest* 1929, *The Dain* Curse 1929, *The Maltese Falcon* 1930, *The Glass Key* 1931, *The Thin Man* 1934) into a reluctant detective.

Cook's was a nothing part that seemed included for nostalgic fondness. *The Maltese Falcon* was Elijah Cook Jr.'s second noir. The circle was complete. We farewelled the man of a thousand humiliations.

Returned war hero Sterling Hayden appeared before the House Un-American Activities Committee HUAC on April 10, 1951. It was humiliating for the progressive former briefly communist Hayden.

By this time, he had three film noirs under his belt.

Distraught: Hayden testifies before the HUAC.

Speaking to his psychiatrist, he said "I don't think you have the foggiest notion of the contempt I have had for myself since the day I did that thing (naming former Communist Party members).

Hayden's first noir *Manhandled* 1949 was a confusing tale, not helped by cartoonish publicity. Women falling for a heel who steps on them is right up there with the corniest of taglines.

Hayden's second noir was the heist classic *The Asphalt Jungle* 1950, directed by John Huston. Hayden is pictured with Jean Hagen.

Though it has come to be regarded as a great noir, it only recorded a profit of $40, 000 on a $1.2 million budget. This may have explained the initial reluctance of United Artists to support Kubrick's pitch to have Hayden as the lead in *The Killing*.

Sunset: Hagen and Hayden ride off into the sunset – of their dreams.

BERNHARD PRODUCTIONS
Presents

JOURNEY
INTO
LIGHT

STERLING HAYDEN · VIVECA LINDFORS · THOMAS MITCHELL
LUDWIG DONATH · H. B. WARNER · JANE DARWELL
STUART HEISLER · JOSEPH BERNHARD · ANSON BOND
ANSON BOND · STEPHANIE NORDLI and IRVING SHULMAN

20
CENTURY-FOX

Journey into Light 1951 is a strange noir exploring the dissolution and redemption of a religious Minister, played by Hayden. *The Killing* cinematographer Elwood Bredell shot this one. Hayden was hoping to avoid a journey into the darkness of an HUAC appearance.

The man who would go on to play paranoid conspiracy theorist General Jack D. Ripper in Kubrick's *Dr. Strangelove* 1964 co-operated with the FBI that was supporting the HUAC, though he was reluctant to do so. "Some of the best creative people were . . . driven out of the industry . . . writers, producers, directors. These days the town is running scared."
(Hayden, S. *Wanderer* Bantam Books by arrangement with Alfred A. Knopf N.Y. 1964, p. 243)

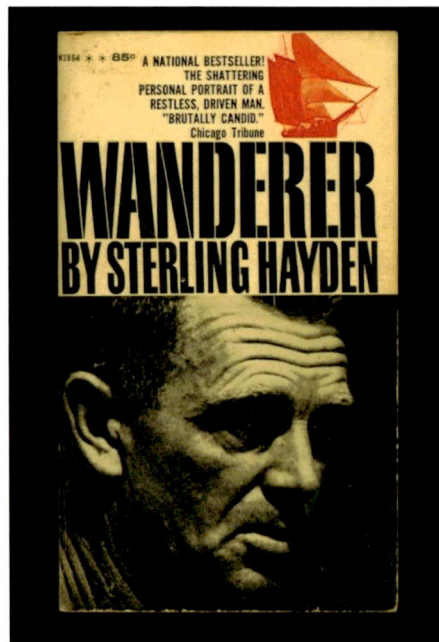

In his autobiography *Wanderer* 1964 Hayden recounts monologues to his therapist. "I'm in plenty of trouble, Doc; haven't worked in a long time. John Huston over at MGM is interested in me for the lead role (in *The Asphalt Jungle*). Doc, I've got to get this part. Don't you want to help me and get rid of me and go on to somebody else?"
"I am afraid our time is up for today." (Hayden *Wanderer*, pp. 340-41).

Cold Warrior: J. Edgar Hoover

After good notices for *The Asphalt Jungle*, Hayden expected to get film offers but he discovered he was graylisted, unofficially blacklisted. His therapist advised him the FBI would respect his confidence if he accepted their request for an interview at which he named names of suspected Communist Party members or sympathisers. "If it hadn't been for you, I never would have been a stoolie for J. Edgar Hoover," Hayden told his therapist. (Hayden, *Wanderer*, p. 354).

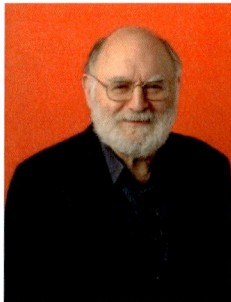

Degrade:
Since it had the names it was asking for, what I conclude is that it was a ritual they were asking people to go through, and the anthropologists call that kind of ritual a 'degradation ceremony'.
– Navasky to Studs Terkel, Dec. 1980.

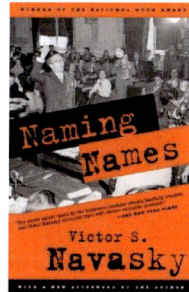

One person Hayden does not name is his therapist. *Naming Names* author Victor S. Navasky, pictured, believed he was Phil Cohen, a former Communist Party member and a practicing therapist without psychoanalytical qualifications.

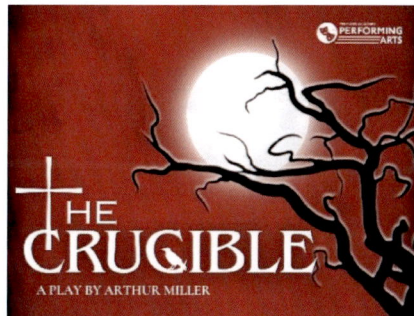

Navasky speculated Cohen might have been an informer for the FBI which Cohen denied to the author. Pictured above is the promotion for the 2024 student production at Thetford Academy, Norfolk England, of Arthur Miller's allegory of the HUAC and contemporaneous McCarthy hearings. Students and teachers considered it timely to revive *The Crucible*.

If Cohen was his therapist, Hayden said to him, "I don't think you have the foggiest notion of the contempt I have had for myself since the day I did that thing."

(Hayden *Wanderer*, p. 354).

NAMELESS, SHAMELESS WOMAN!

TRAINED IN AN ART AS OLD AS TIME! She served a mob of terror
and violence whose one mission is to destroy! Trading her love...
yielding kisses that invite disaster, destroy...then — KILL!

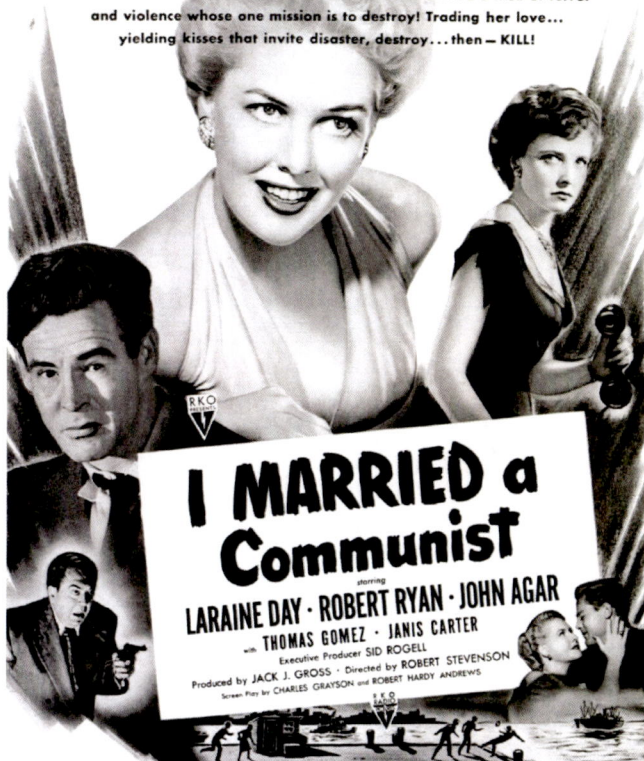

I MARRIED a Communist

starring
LARAINE DAY · ROBERT RYAN · JOHN AGAR
with THOMAS GOMEZ · JANIS CARTER
Executive Producer SID ROGELL
Produced by JACK J. GROSS · Directed by ROBERT STEVENSON
Screen Play by CHARLES GRAYSON and ROBERT HARDY ANDREWS

The HUAC wanted Hayden to star in their anti-communist show trial. We do not know whether the FBI and Hayden reached an agreement, but all Hayden copped to before the HUAC was five or six months of inactive membership of the Hollywood Independent Citizens Committee of the Arts Science and Professions (HICCASP}.

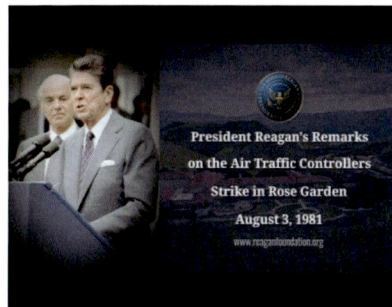

President Reagan's Remarks
on the Air Traffic Controllers
Strike in Rose Garden
August 3, 1981
www.reaganfoundation.org

The FBI regarded HICCASP as a communist-front organisation but its membership at various times included Humphrey Bogart, Charlie Chaplin, Rita Hayworth, Charles Laughton, director Irving Pichel, scientist Linus Pauling (pictured at his 1922 graduation) Orson Welles, and Ronald Reagan.

That's right, future Republican President, Ronald Reagan, a liberal at the time, was a member of an organisation which the FBI regarded as a communist front. In 1968, Reagan fired 11,345 striking air traffic controllers and banned them from federal service for life.

Inhuman Pinkos: The HUAC dehumanizes to describe communists. **Inset:** Cousin Itt from the television sitcom *The Addams Family* 1965-6.

Hayden told the HUAC on April 10, 1951, he wanted it known that no one coerced him into joining HICCASP. Then he added, with the utmost sincerity something strange. "It was the stupidest, most ignorant thing I have ever done, and I have done a good many such things."

Who knows? Maybe Hayden rehearsed that line. Ran it by *The Asphalt Jungle* director, John Huston. Hayden was not blacklisted and six of his movies, no noirs, were released in 1952.

Hayden's next noir *Crime Wave* 1954, directed by Andre De Toth, featured the debut of Charles Bronson, billed as Charles Buchinsky.

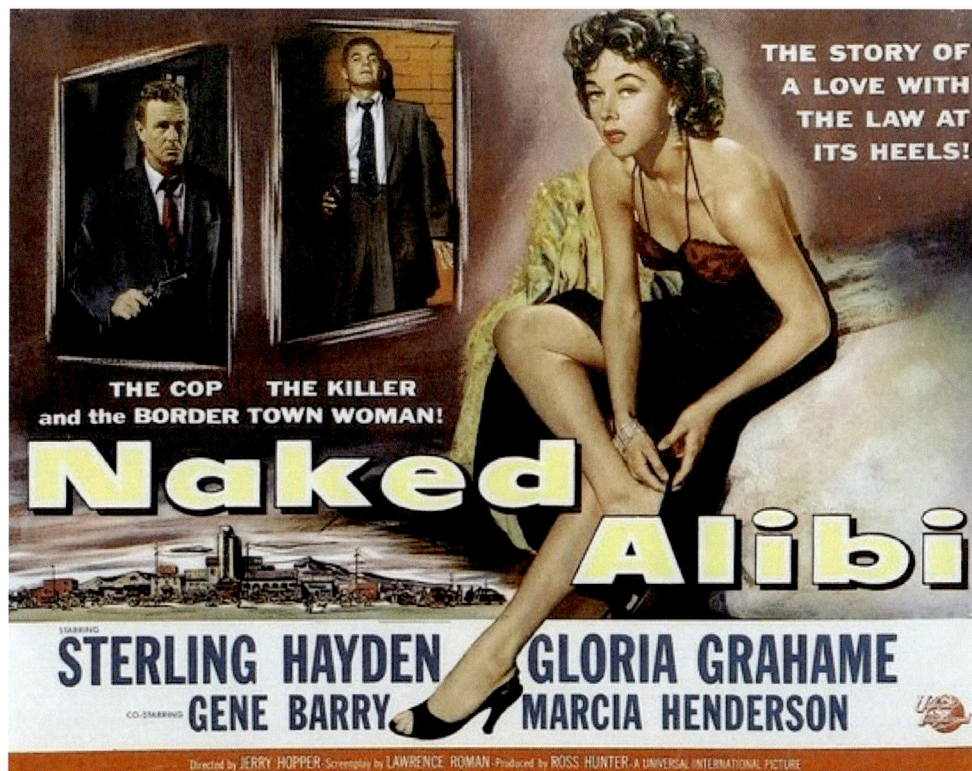

THE STORY OF A LOVE WITH THE LAW AT ITS HEELS!

THE COP THE KILLER and the BORDER TOWN WOMAN!

Naked Alibi

STARRING
STERLING HAYDEN GLORIA GRAHAME
CO-STARRING GENE BARRY MARCIA HENDERSON

Directed by JERRY HOPPER · Screenplay by LAWRENCE ROMAN · Produced by ROSS HUNTER · A UNIVERSAL INTERNATIONAL PICTURE

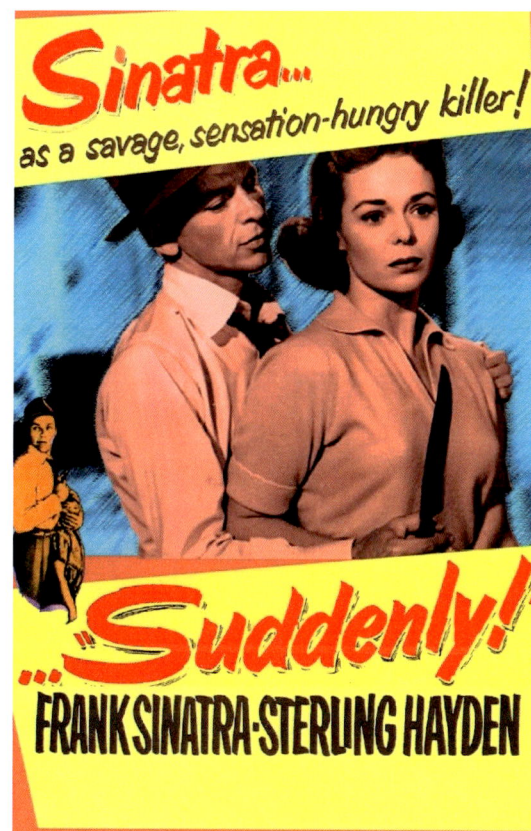

Sinatra...
as a savage, sensation-hungry killer!

..."Suddenly!"
FRANK SINATRA · STERLING HAYDEN

Good in part: Hayden had a good role in the tough noir *Naked Alibi*. But he was shortchanged by the writers of *Suddenly* who gave him a dull character in a lively film.

Neither movie lived up to the salacity suggested in the title of *Naked Alibi* or the tagline portraying the Sinatra character as savage and lewd.

As with *Crime Wave* his two other 1954 noirs saw Hayden playing a law enforcement officer including the cold war noir *Suddenly* with Frank Sinatra playing a traitor. Perhaps Hayden and his agent decided it was smart to give up outlaw roles for a while. *Naked Alibi* is a good movie.

ANNE
BAXTER
STERLING
HAYDEN

ALLIED ARTISTS

with JOHN HOYT · JESSE WHITE

SUPERSCOPE

A LINDSLEY PARSONS
PRODUCTION

DIRECTED BY
RUSSELL BIRDWELL

The Come On

Besides *The Killing*, Hayden's other 1956 noir was the "try-hard, no prize" *The Come On*. Academy Award winner Anne Baxter (*The Razor's Edge* 1946) had an excuse for being in the movie as her partner Russell Birdwell directed. Hayden might have smoked too much weed before signing on.

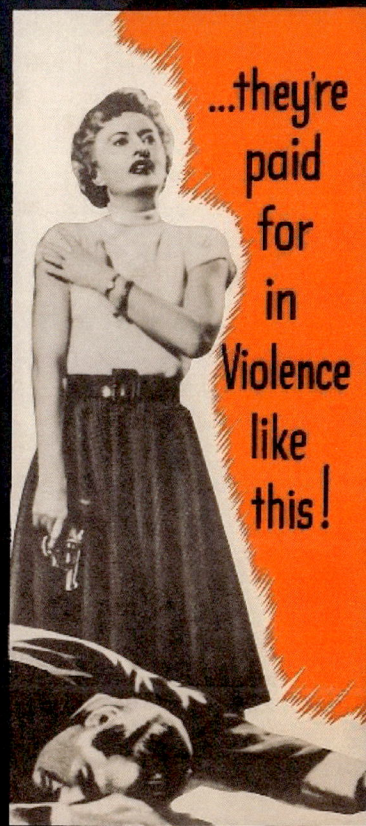

RUTH ROMAN   STERLING HAYDEN

FIVE STEPS TO DANGER

The year 1957 started with another police officer role, this time in the good noir *Crime of Passion* that was undervalued by critics at its time of release. Hayden followed this with another cold war noir co-starring Ruth Roman. The *Five Steps to Danger* are unexplained. They could have been when two good actors entered the studio to make this film.

That was it. Sterling Hayden left the dwindling noir universe and only returned for one last shot in the neo-noir *The Long Goodbye* 1973, directed by Robert Altman.

The verdict *The Killing*

★★★★☆

After the embarrassing (by Kubrick's own assessment) sloppiness of *Fear and Desire*, Kubrick decided to make a film noir that became *Killer's Kiss*. One advantage of noir was the genre structure that Kubrick's first feature lacked. Another plus was the tradition of low budgets. A third was that noir's lineage gave it potential for the artistry the filmmaker had botched in *Fear and Desire*. Kubrick's third feature was also a noir, recognized today as a significant one. Two noirs laid the path to cinematic glory.

1957

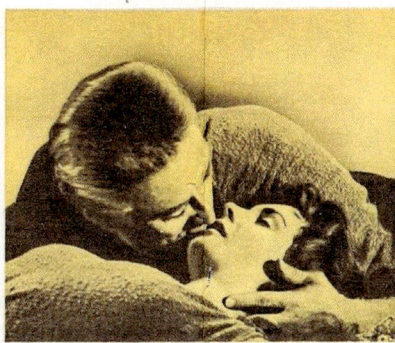

1960

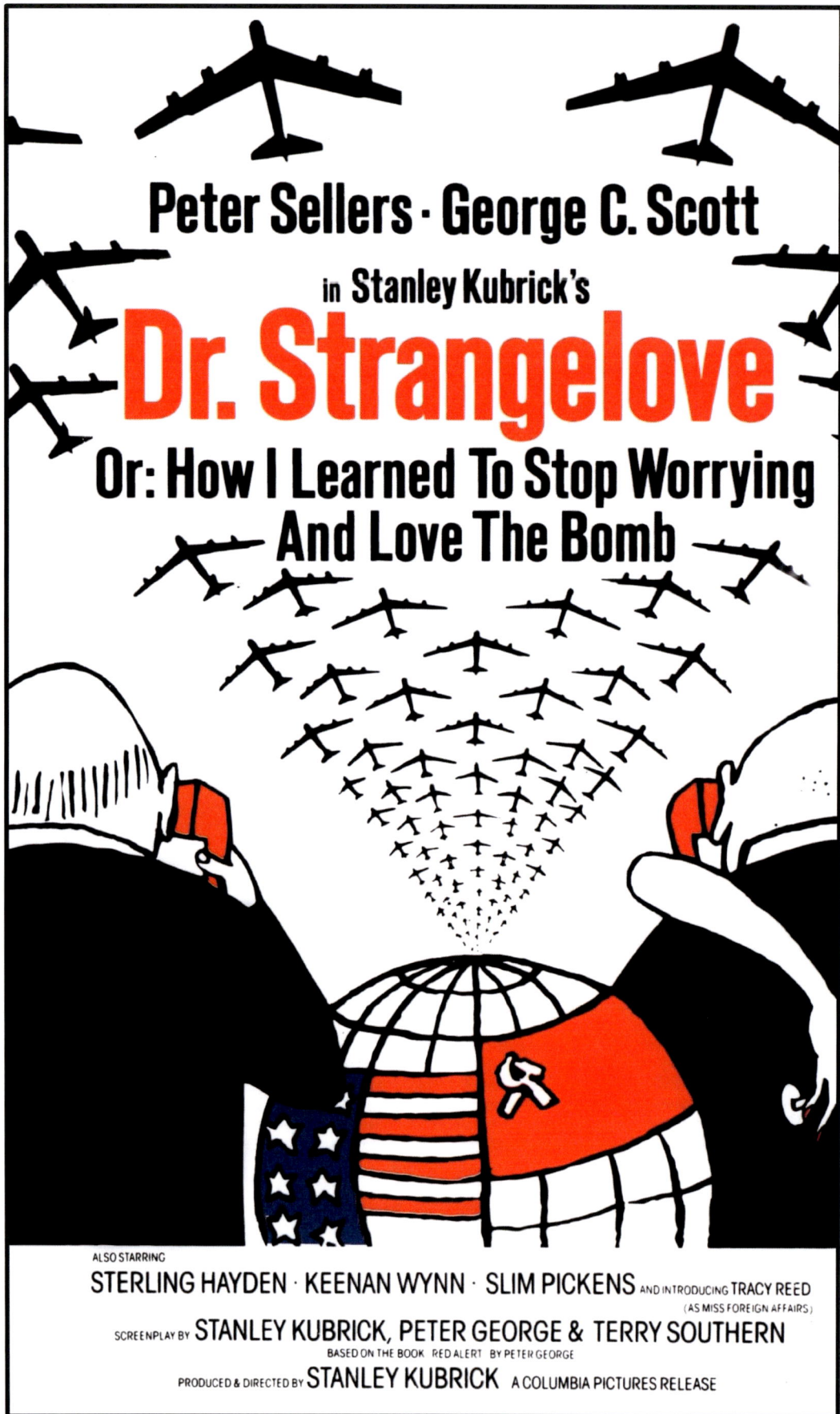

Peter Sellers · George C. Scott

in Stanley Kubrick's

Dr. Strangelove

Or: How I Learned To Stop Worrying And Love The Bomb

ALSO STARRING
STERLING HAYDEN · KEENAN WYNN · SLIM PICKENS AND INTRODUCING TRACY REED
(AS MISS FOREIGN AFFAIRS)
SCREENPLAY BY STANLEY KUBRICK, PETER GEORGE & TERRY SOUTHERN
BASED ON THE BOOK RED ALERT BY PETER GEORGE
PRODUCED & DIRECTED BY STANLEY KUBRICK A COLUMBIA PICTURES RELEASE

1964

1965

STANLEY KUBRICK'S

CLOCKWORK ORANGE

1971

1980

IN VIETNAM
THE WIND
DOESN'T BLOW
IT SUCKS

BORN TO KILL

Stanley Kubrick's

FULL
METAL
JACKET

WARNER BROS PRESENTS STANLEY KUBRICK'S FULL METAL JACKET

STARRING
MATTHEW MODINE ADAM BALDWIN VINCENT D'ONOFRIO LEE ERMEY DORIAN HAREWOOD ARLISS HOWARD

KEVYN MAJOR HOWARD ED O'ROSS SCREENPLAY BY STANLEY KUBRICK MICHAEL HERR GUSTAV HASFORD

BASED ON THE NOVEL THE SHORT-TIMERS BY GUSTAV HASFORD CO PRODUCER PHILIP HOBBS EXECUTIVE PRODUCER JAN HARLAN PRODUCED AND DIRECTED BY STANLEY KUBRICK

WARNER BROS A WARNER COMMUNICATIONS COMPANY
1987 Warner Bros. Inc. All Rights Reserved.

1987

164

Kubrick's three other feature films were more critically and popularly contentious regarding their excellence:

1962

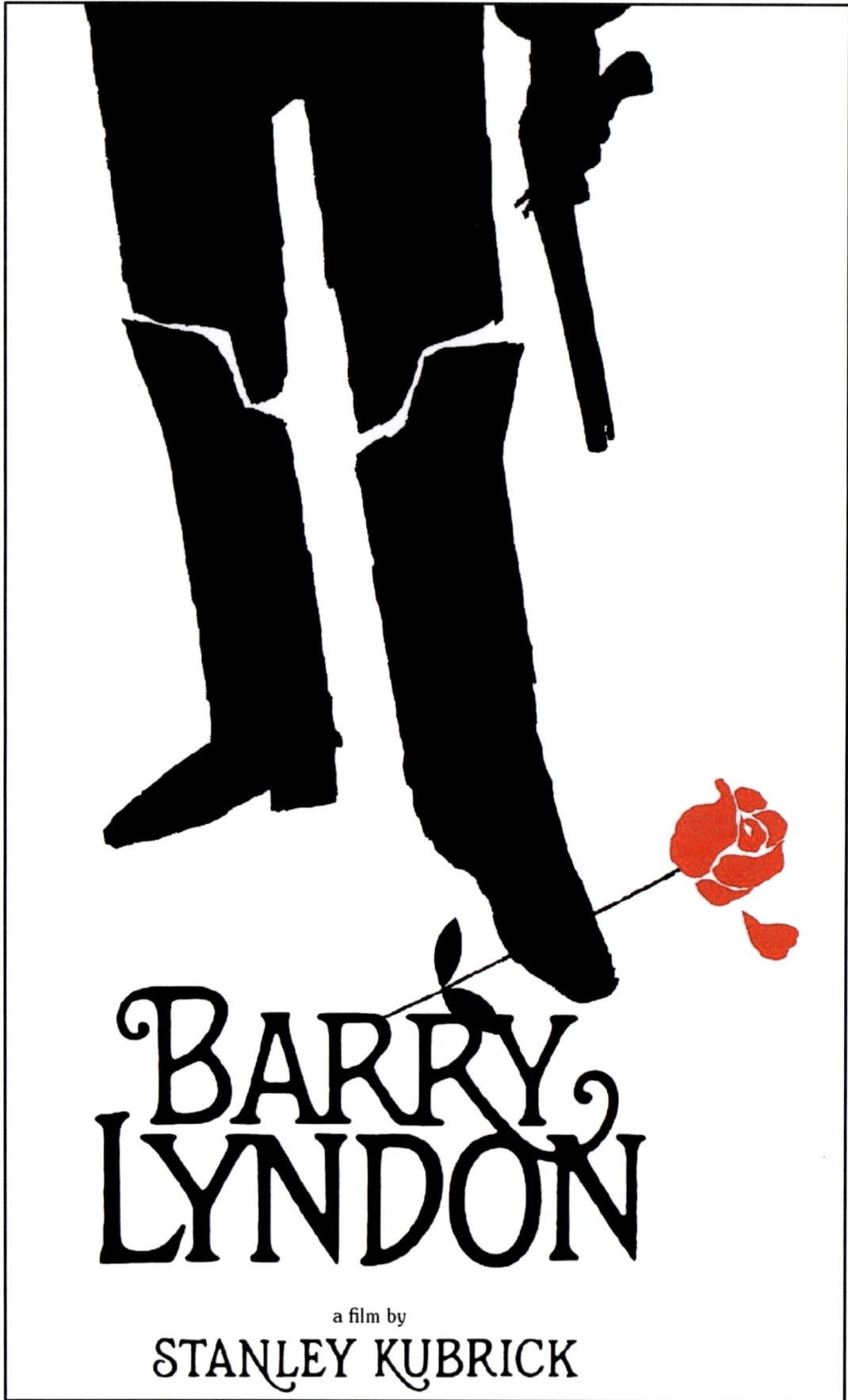

BARRY LYNDON

a film by
STANLEY KUBRICK

1975

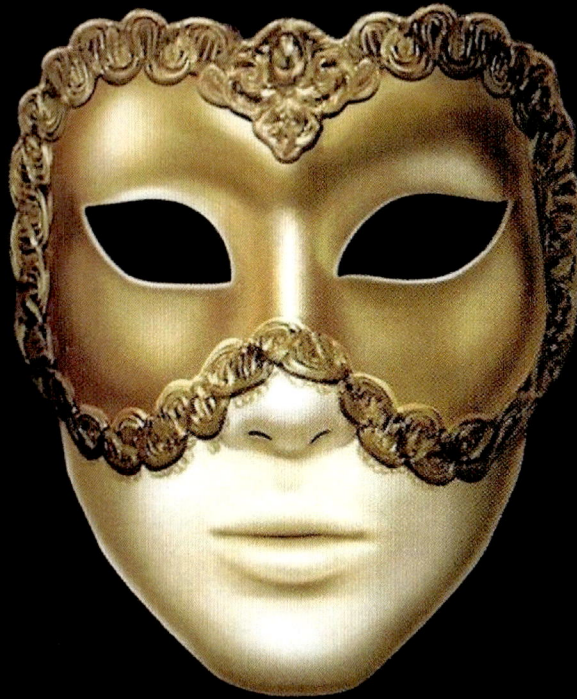

STANLEY KUBRICK'S

eyes wide

shut

WARNER BROS. PRESENTS

TOM CRUISE, NICOLE KIDMAN IN A FILM BY STANLEY KUBRICK "EYES WIDE SHUT" SYDNEY POLLACK, MARIE RICHARDSON, RADE SHERBEDGIA SCREENPLAY BY STANLEY KUBRICK AND FREDERIC RAPHAEL INSPIRED BY "TRAUMNOVELLE" BY ARTHUR SCHNITZLER EXECUTIVE PRODUCER JAN HARLAN LIGHTING CAMERAMAN LARRY SMITH PRODUCTION DESIGNERS LES TOMKINS, ROY WALKER EDITOR NIGEL GALT PRODUCED AND DIRECTED BY STANLEY KUBRICK Soundtrack Album on Warner Sunset/Reprise Records

eyeswideshut.com   warnervideo.com

WARNER BROS. PICTURES A WARNER BROS. ENTERTAINMENT COMPANY

1999

Lolita and Barry Lyndon have been critically rehabilitated. Kubrick's last film, Eyes Wide Shut, completed weeks before his death, still divides critics and viewers. Just between us, in camera, Me Leica.

Cringe 1946

WHAT really annoys me about amateur book reviewers is when they say they don't like the characters. I mean, did Bret Easton Ellis expect you to like the characters of *American Psycho?* After watching *The Strange Woman,* I can understand the criticism against unlikable characters.

The Strange Woman is a good film, well directed by Edgar G. Ulmer and well photographed by Lucien Andriot. The acting is more than adequate. But the main characters are without exception as unattractive a bunch as are likely to cross a screen before you. This makes the movie less engrossing as the viewer is less invested in hoping protagonists are saved from the inevitable noir calamities.

Humiliated by growing up in poverty with a physically abusive single father, Jenny Hagan (Lamarr) decides to barter her beauty for material comfort after her father dies. Whether she is intent on taking revenge against all men as substitutes for her Dad is for the viewer to decide.

The opening credits offer little guidance of what is to follow. They are in a flowery font suggesting a period romance when what is in store is a harrowing period noir. I suspect the filmmakers intended to fool viewers and thus make the film more memorable.

The movie itself begins with a scene with children which is important to explain the actions of the adults they become. This technique is unusual for noir but is effective here and in *The Strange Love of Martha Ivers* 1946 which is a superior film to *The Strange Woman*.

You will notice the word "strange" in both titles. "Strange Woman" is a Biblical reference, quoted in the Lamarr film by travelling fire-and-brimstone evangelist Lincoln Pittridge (Ian Keith). "The lips of a strange woman drip honey, and her mouth is smoother than oil. But her end is bitter as wormwood, sharp as a two-edged sword!" A reference to venereal disease seems to have slipped past the censors.

Strange in the Bible refers to a seducer or prostitute though the notion of stranger or outsider (travelling prostitutes) is also there. Jenny Hagar uses her sexuality to enter wealthy sanctimonious upper-middle-class society.

Cold of heart: Lamarr with spurned lover Louis Hayward.

The Player

The Strange Woman was the 16th Hollywood film of Austrian-born **HEDY LAMARR** who was deprived of lines in her early films by producers and directors who discounted her talent. In *The Strange Woman*, she gives a superior performance though she does not display the redeeming features of a great femme fatale. Director Edgar G. Ulmer had relative success the previous year with his low-budget noir *Detour* 1945 which returned multiples of its budget of under $100,000 ($1.7m in 2025 values). The character of femme fatale Vera was nuanced.

Director Ulmer praised Lamarr's work. "It nearly got Hedy Lamarr an Academy nomination," Ulmer said. "It's the only picture where she ever had to act." (Bogdanovich, P. *Who the Hell Made It*, Ballantine Books eBook, p. 898). Ulmer is praising himself for extracting a performance from Lamarr. It is always about the auteur. That's the way they roll them.

The success of *Detour* prompted *The Strange Woman* producer Lamarr to hire Ulmer and provide him with a much larger budget which ended up exceeded by $1m ($17m in 2025 value). What Ulmer managed to do in *Detour* was to assist in the creation of the definitive femme fatale in Vera (played by unknown Ann Savage). With a much bigger budget to have exploding fires, runaway carriages, and river rapids ravaging canoes, Ulmer and Lamarr are unable to conjure the nuances of the good and evil of a classic femme fatale as Savage did. Even when Jenny (Lamarr) performs virtuous deeds, giving money for children's education and poverty relief, her motives are self-centred on her own cringey childhood, and we remember her atrocious acts. Unfortunately, the poster premise of a good and evil femme fatale is unfulfilled. *The Strange Woman* at times has the ambience of an up-market exploitation film.

171

Character actor **GENE LOCKHART** as creepy merchant Isaiah Poster has an extended role in the film and takes the acting honors. The close-up of Poster leering at Lamarr's exposed shoulder is one highlight of the film.

Gene Lockhart was in more than 300 movies, and he received a supporting Academy Award for *Algiers*. An actor playing a despicable character in a support role has had a chance of picking up an Academy Award. Examples around this time were Gale Sondergaard (in her film debut) *Anthony Adverse* 1936, Thomas Mitchell *Stagecoach* 1940, Mary Astor *The Great Lie* 1941, and Walter Brennan *The Westerner* 1941.

Baddie once more: Lockhart was still a villain in 1954's *World for Ransom*, starring Dan Duryea and directed by Robert Aldrich. The movie is a good ultra cheapie.

Lockhart's other noirs included *Hangmen Also Die* 1943, *The House on 92nd Street* 1945, *Leave Her to Heaven* 1945, *Red Light* 1949, *Hoodlum Empire* 1952, and *World for Ransom* 1954. Lockhart performed in six more films after *World for Ransom* before he died in 1957.

Another outstanding performance in a smaller part is that of **OLIVE BLAKENEY** as Mrs. Hollis, the compassionate but surprisingly worldly-wise housekeeper. Mrs. Hollis understands the lascivious intent of the sanctimonious hypocrite Isaiah Poster and wants to protect young Jenny from him.

Blakeney had a role in the 1944 noir *The Port of Forty Thieves* and an uncredited part *in Leave Her to Heaven*.

She was with Hedy Lamarr in *Experiment Perilous*, directed by Jacques Tourneur. Blakeney was again uncredited for *I Want to Live* 1958, for which the Lead Susan Hayward won the Academy Award.

KATHLEEN LOCKHART who plays Mrs. Partridge was in real life the wife of Gene Lockhart and the mother of June Lockhart who was in television hits *Lassie* 1954-73 and *Lost in Space* 1965-68.

June Lockhart was the female lead in the film *Son of Lassie* 1945. Peter Lawford was the male lead, if you did not count Pal, the third actor in the photo. Male Rough Collie Pal played Lassie in four movies. He played Laddie son of Lassie, and Bill, also related to Lassie, in *Courage of Lassie* 1946. Playing Bill, Pal was billed as Lassie. Hollywood is a weird town.

June's daughter Anne Lockhart was a pre-teen when she made five uncredited guest appearances in TV *Lassie*.

As an adult Anne appeared in *Happy Days* 1975, *Barnaby Jones* 1977, and *Project U.F.O.* 1978 before 12 episodes of *Battlestar Galactica* 1978-9. Kathleen Lockhart, Gene and June, were in *A Christmas Carol* 1938.

Battlestar dress-ups: Anne Lockhart, Patrick Macnee *The Avengers* 1961–1969, and Lorne Greene *Bonanza* 1959-73.

Franco-American **LUCIEN ANDRIOT** photographed more than 200 films, mostly on modest budgets. Andriot shot all genres and styles of film, and he was active in silents from 1915.

He shot *Charlie Chan at the Opera*, 1936 starring Warner Oland for the 13th time as the Chinese detective, and featuring Boris *Frankenstein* Karloff as, of all roles, an opera singer. One line from the campy movie is, "This opera is going on tonight, even if Frankenstein walks in."

After *The Strange Woman*, Andriot shot *Dishonored Lady* 1947, *Johnny One-Eye* 1950, and *Borderline* 1950.

Andriot shot *The Southerner* 1945. Director Jean Renoir was nominated for an Oscar. Robert Aldrich was the assistant director. ★★★★☆

A good line and a weird one

Jenny Hagar (Lamarr) to her father: "Men like me and it's the men who have the money in this world."

Tim Hager (Dennis Hoey) who is about to take a stockwhip to his daughter: "This is one beating you won't like."
What are you insinuating there, Dad?

British actor Hoey played Inspector Lestrade in six Universal Studio Sherlock Holmes films from 1942-46.

The verdict *The Strange Woman*

★★★⯪☆

Thanks for watching

Epilogue

An epilogue is an addendum to a book that brings closure. As this is the fourth and final volume of this series, I will give my favorite 10 film noirs.

My books in paperback and hardback are, by necessity, not cheap to make or buy. During this series, I have tried to value-add the service of alerting the reader to films, including hidden gems, worth watching.

#10 Neo-noir

1998

A Simple Plan is a throwback to the days of B-noirs. It was filmed over 55 days (admittedly eight films' worth at PRC) on a budget of $17 million. The characterizations of the ensemble cast are superb with Billy Bob Thornton deservedly receiving an Oscar nomination.

It suffers from a common affliction of post 1980 noirs, excessive violence, but it is so brilliant you must forgive it that.

Set in rural Minnesota, it reminds me a little of *Storm Fear* 1955 in its reaffirmation that film noir is not strictly an urban genre.

1932

This one is controversial. Many critics do not regard *Rain* as a proto-noir. For most of her career, Joan Crawford said her performance stank though she did the right thing by herself and blamed director Lewis Milestone who, she claimed, left her directionless.

I regard *Rain* as a noir with superb performances from Crawford and Walter Huston. Milestone's direction and photography by Oliver T. Marsh (*San Francisco* 1936) are near faultless.

The themes of misogyny, sublimated sexuality, and religious totalitarianism are timeless.

1947

Glad you could join us for our fabulous Mademoiselle Femme Fatale contest. In third place is Miss Gloria Grahame for *Sudden Fear* 1952. In second place is Miss Lizabeth Scott for *Too Late for Tears* 1949. To crown Ms Scott is her doting uncle, Mr. Dan Duryea. And the winner is . . .

. . . Miss Jane Greer is the iconic femme fatale in *Out of the Past*, cool and beautiful but in distress. Or is she? Sleepy-eyed Robert Mitchum is about to find out. Fate always cooks up an evil plan when It sees Mitchum lumbering along. Kirk Douglas is Fate's demonic instrument.

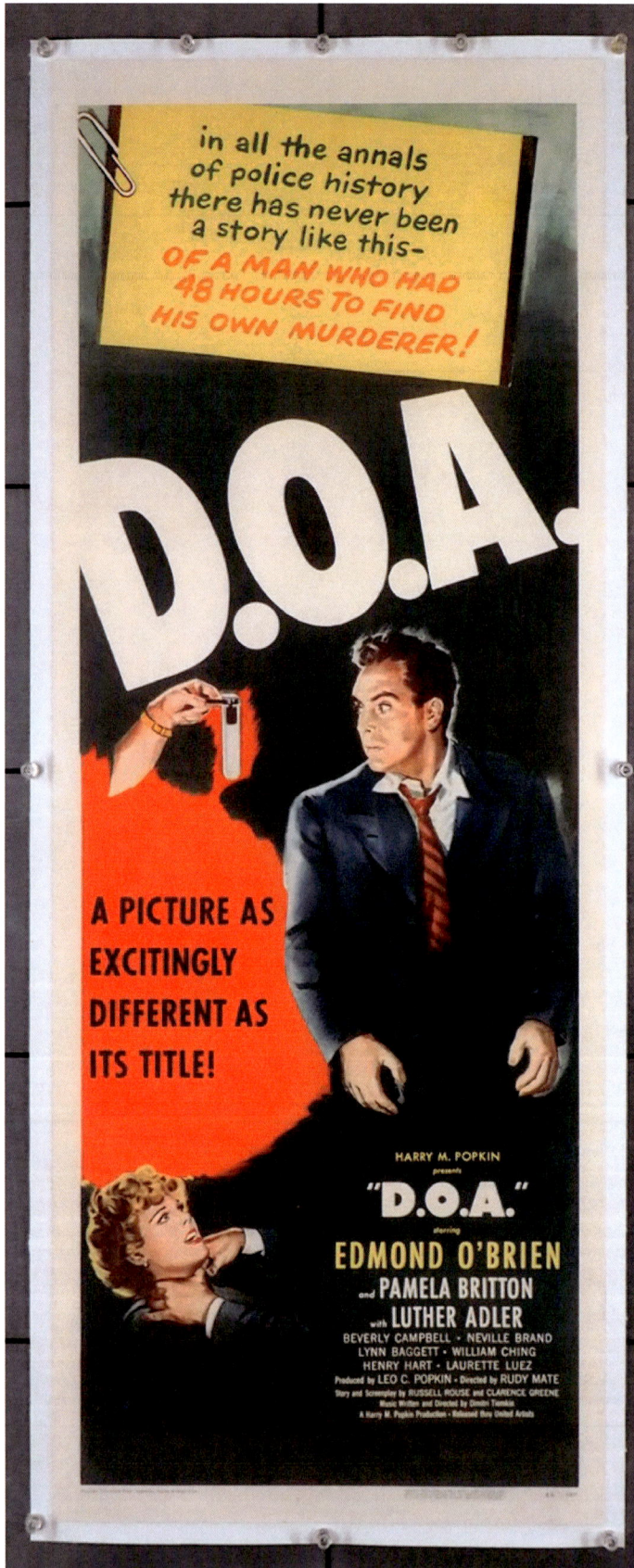

D.O.A. is the total picture with:
an inspired beginning,
sharp direction from Rudolph Maté,
mood shooting by Ernest Laszlo, and
great supports in Neville Brand and
Luther Adler.

This low-budget gem proves money
can't buy a lovely movie.

1950

1946

You knew it would be in my Top 10 somewhere.

It contains two of my favorite noir scenes – Bogie and Dorothy Malone flirting in the bookshop, and Bob Steele confronting Elisha Cook Jr. at the water cooler.

Hard-boiled noir is peppered with sophisticated humor.

1941

One of the many reasons *The Big Sleep* and *The Maltese Falcon* became great films was that directors Howard Hawks and John Huston were loyal to the source novels of Raymond Chandler and Dashiell Hammett. In my estimation, Chandler was funnier, and Hammett was the better writer. As for the quality of their film versions, I cannot separate them.

A FILM BY
AKIRA KUROSAWA
WITH
TOSHIRO MIFUNE
TAKASHI SHIMURA

野良犬

STRAY
DOG

DIRECTED BY AKIRA KUROSAWA
PRODUCED BY SŌJIRŌ MOTOKI
WRITTEN BY AKIRA KUROSAWA | RYŪZŌ KIKUSHIMA
STARRING TOSHIRO MIFUNE | TAKASHI SHIMURA
MUSIC BY FUMIO HAYASAKA
CINEMATOGRAPHY ASAKAZU NAKAI
EDITED BY TOSHIO GOTŌ |YOSHI SUGIHARA

1949

Japanese auteur Akira Kurosawa had the rare gift of making intellectual films that appealed to a wide audience. *Stray Dog* has the ambience of a Hollywood noir while it explores post-war deprivation and subjugation of Japanese culture under American occupation. Such discussions in cultural products were specifically banned by American military censors but the genius Kurosawa slipped this movie past them.

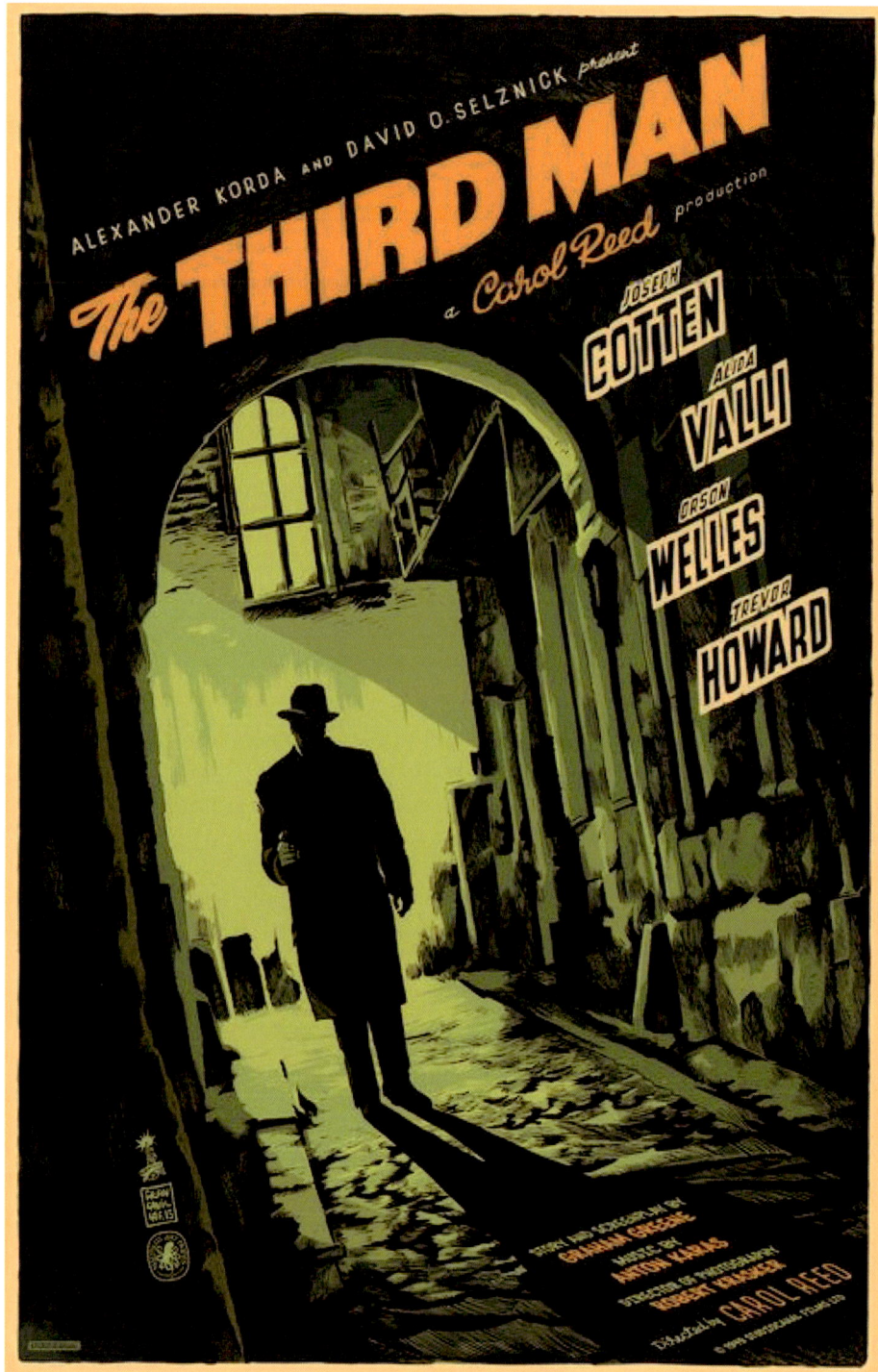

1949

Critics believe this British film is the greatest noir of all time. Even if you do not agree, it would be disrespectful to argue against it.

The cinematography of Robert Krasker borders on the extraordinary. Carol Reed's direction is compelling. It was Reed who thought out of the box to include the versatile zither music of Anton Karas. Joseph Cotten and Alida Valli deliver poignantly under-stated performances while Orson Welles, larger than life, bounds across the screen to dominate his scenes.

1946

This gem is not as widely known as others of my Top 10. Inexplicably, it failed to make Slant magazine's November 2024 list of 100 best noirs. Rotten Tomatoes' Tomatometer ranked it #43. (No, I don't know how it works. I'm a tomato eater, not a Tomatometer reader).

Stanwyck's Martha Ivers is among the great femme fatales, heartless bar for one weakness – she loves Van Heflin who wears a lopsided sardonic sneer for much of the film. Van Heflin is in fine form. In his first film role. Kirk Douglas shines as Stanwyck's weak husband. Lizabeth Scott, in her second movie, turns in the performance of her often under-achieving career, as the beautiful victim of lustful and ambitious men.

Robert Rossen wrote this tough exciting and thoughtful film. He would later be writer/ director of *All the King's Men* 1949 and *The Hustler* 1961.

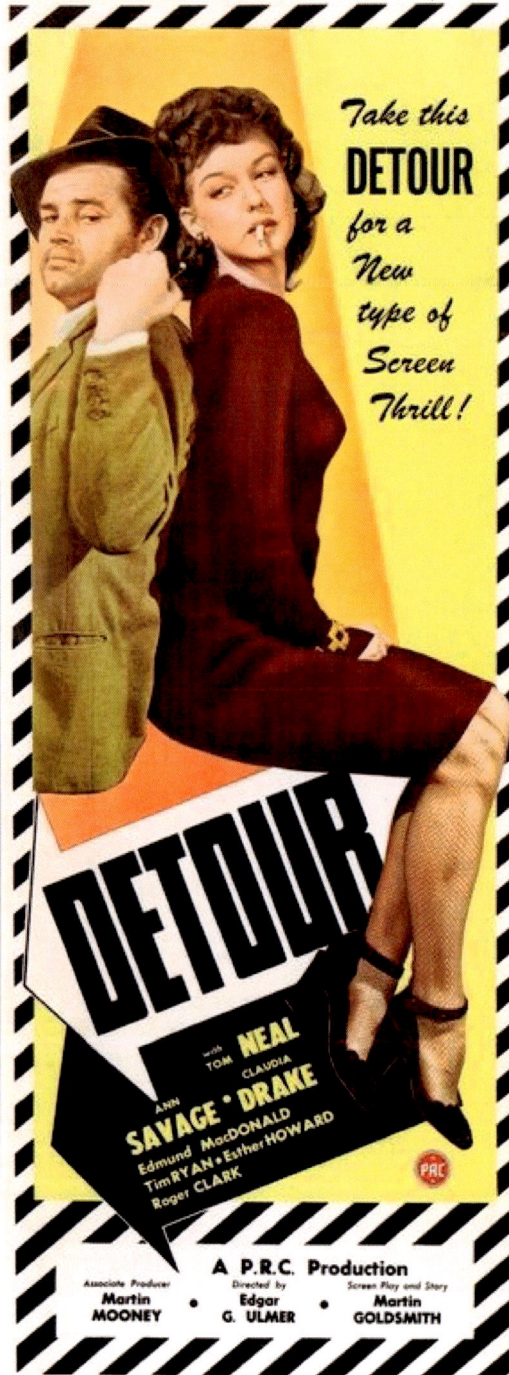

1945

This 1945 B-picture was made for less than $100,000 and returned $1 million, proving that cinema audiences knew how to find a quality cheapie.

Edgar G. Ulmer deftly directs unknown leads Tom Neal (good here but a bad dangerous manchild in real life) and the wonderful Ann Savage.

Benjamin H. Kline's photography is a pleasure to watch and Leo Erdody's score is a joy.

Detour is a great film.

Selected bibliography

Victor S. Navasky

Naming Names

#2884 ** 85¢ A NATIONAL BESTSELLER!
THE SHATTERING
PERSONAL PORTRAIT OF A
RESTLESS, DRIVEN MAN.
"BRUTALLY CANDID."
Chicago Tribune

**WANDERER
BY STERLING HAYDEN**

The Rise and Fall of

Violent Crime in America

BARRY LATZER

WHO THE DEVIL MADE IT

**CONVERSATIONS WITH
LEGENDARY FILM DIRECTORS**

• ROBERT ALDRICH • GEORGE CUKOR • ALLAN DWAN • HOWARD HAWKS •
• ALFRED HITCHCOCK • CHUCK JONES • FRITZ LANG • JOSEPH H. LEWIS •
• SIDNEY LUMET • LEO McCAREY • OTTO PREMINGER • DON SIEGEL •
• JOSEF von STERNBERG • FRANK TASHLIN • EDGAR G. ULMER • RAOUL WALSH •

"A HUGE AND VALUABLE BOOK... BOGDANOVICH INCLUDES EVERYTHING
HISTORY, TECHNIQUE, GOSSIP, MINUTIAE."
—ROGER EBERT, THE NEW YORK TIMES BOOK REVIEW

PETER BOGDANOVICH

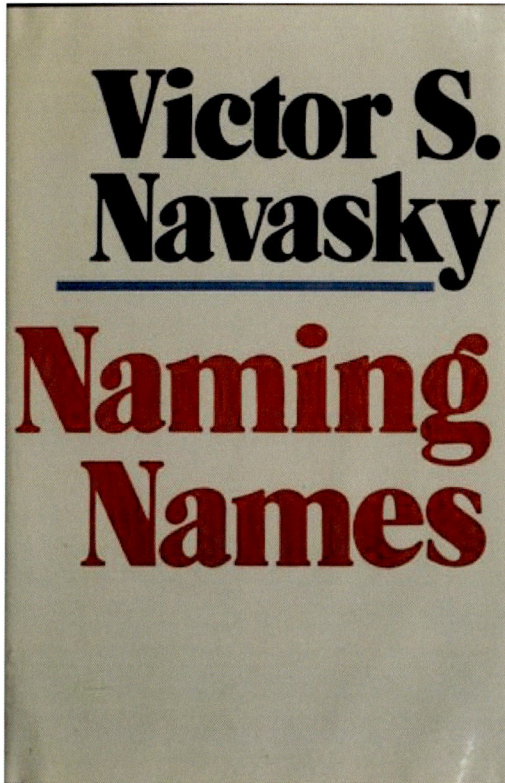

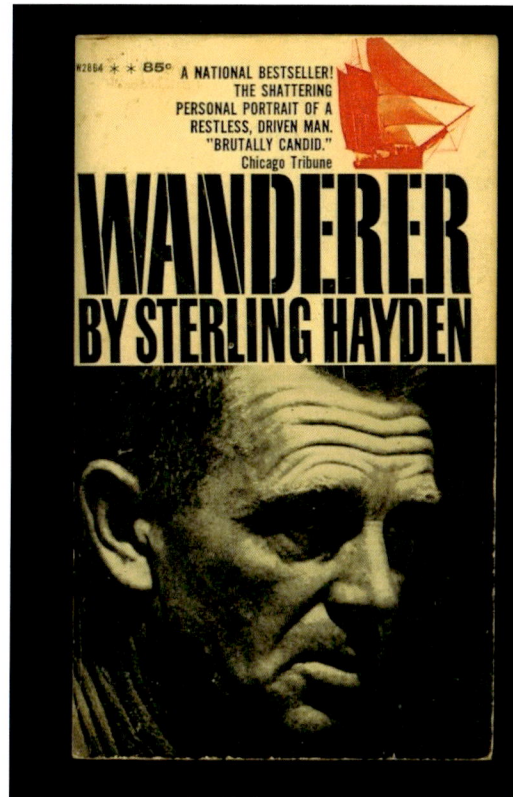

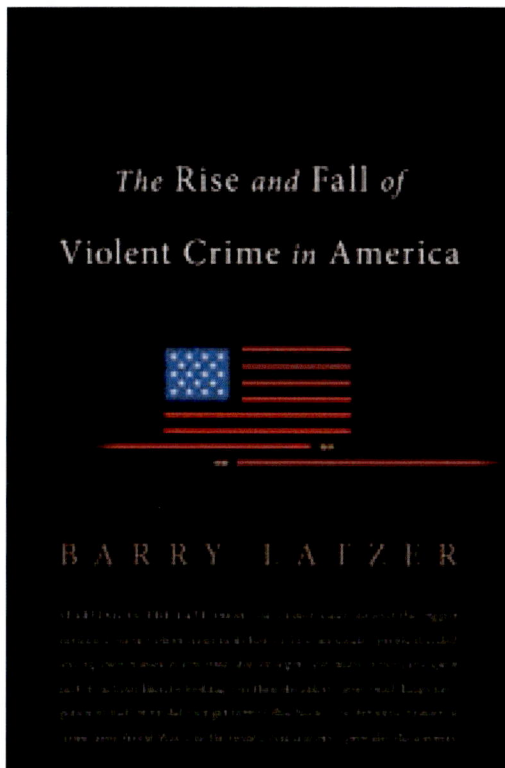

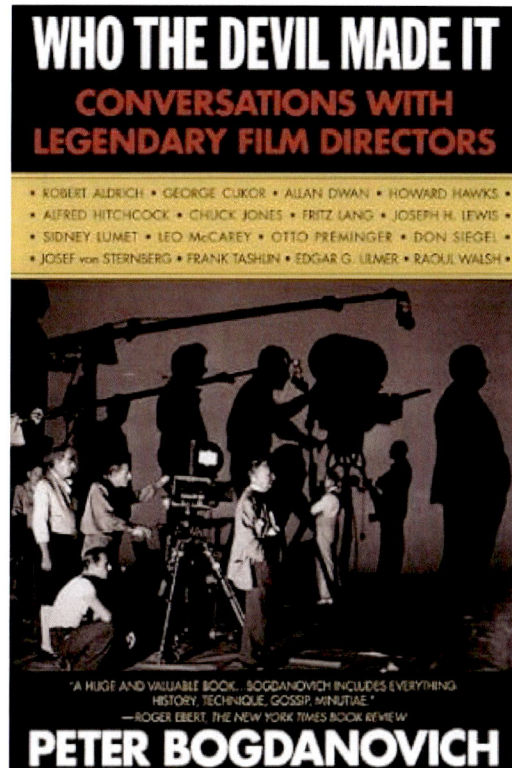

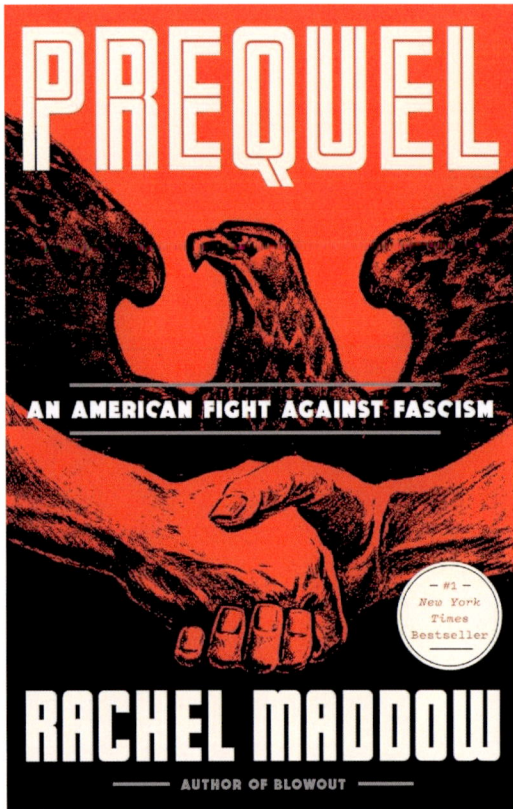

PREQUEL

AN AMERICAN FIGHT AGAINST FASCISM

#1 New York Times Bestseller

RACHEL MADDOW

AUTHOR OF BLOWOUT

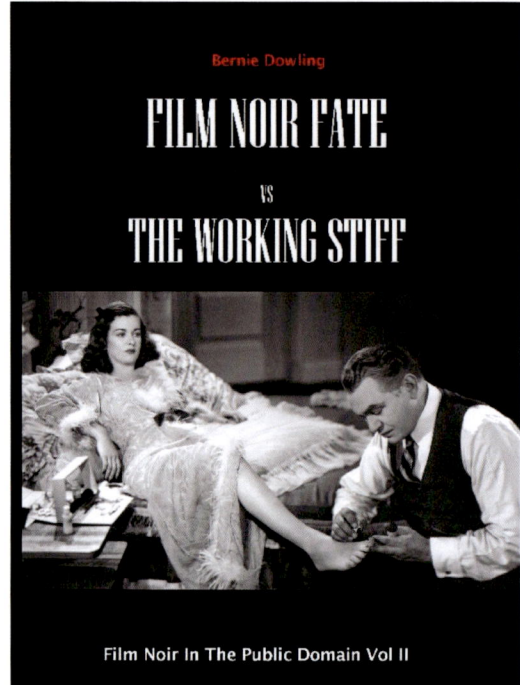

Bernie Dowling

FILM NOIR FATE

VS

THE WORKING STIFF

Film Noir In The Public Domain Vol II

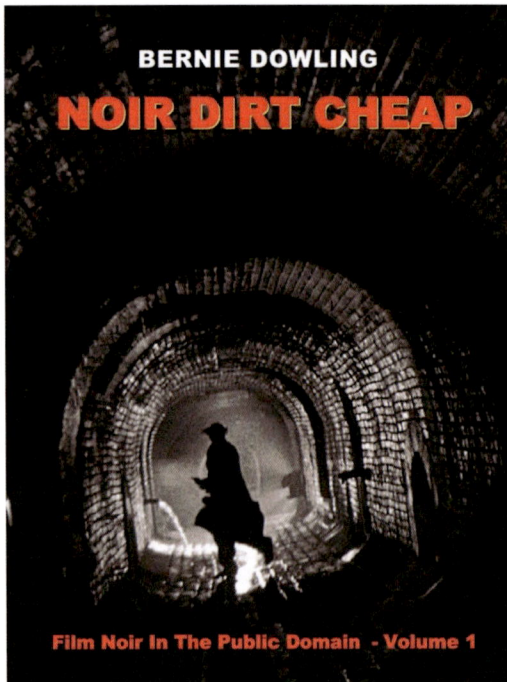

BERNIE DOWLING

NOIR DIRT CHEAP

Film Noir In The Public Domain - Volume 1

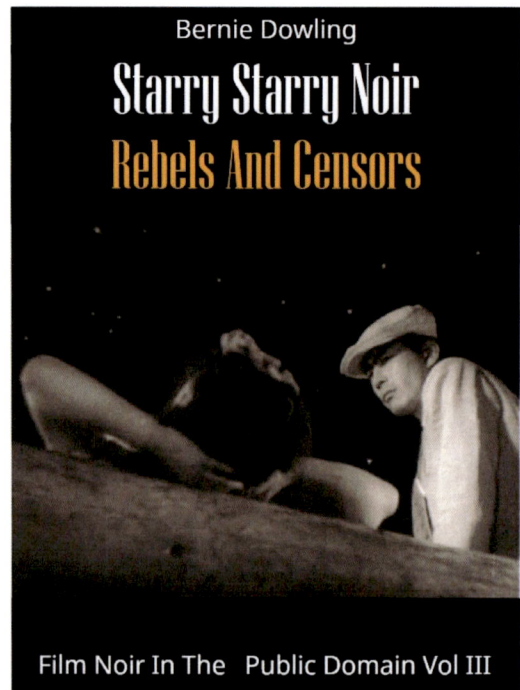

Bernie Dowling

Starry Starry Noir

Rebels And Censors

Film Noir In The   Public Domain Vol III

Y

Z

www.ingramcontent.com/pod-product-compliance
Lightning Source LLC
Chambersburg PA
CBRC101308020426
42333CB00008B/73